DISCOVERING
RICHMOND
MONUMENTS

DISCOVERING
RICHMOND
MONUMENTS

A History of River City Landmarks Beyond the Avenue

ROBERT C. LAYTON

THE
History
PRESS

Published by The History Press
Charleston, SC 29403
www.historypress.net

Copyright © 2013 by Robert C. Layton
All rights reserved

First published 2013

ISBN 978.1.5402.0816.3

Library of Congress CIP data applied for

I dedicate this volume to grandchildren Emma and Caden Burch— may they know the sacrifices that noble men have made so they can live in the greatest country in the world and enjoy the fruits of the labors of those who came before them.

—Bob

To my three favorite Richmond explorers: Mitchell, Carly and my wife, Trish. Thank you.

—Phil

Contents

Prelude, by Paul DiPasquale   9
Acknowledgements   13
Introduction   15

Chapter 1. Downtown   19
Chapter 2. Virginia Commonwealth University   55
Chapter 3. Parks   69
Chapter 4. Military   87
Chapter 5. Law Enforcement   103
Chapter 6. Scattered About the City   111

Appendix I: Symbolism   129
Appendix II: Chronology of Monument and
    Statue Placements in the City   135
Appendix III: The City of Richmond's Public Art Program   141
Appendix IV: Potential Additions to the
    Monuments in Richmond   147
Appendix V: Virginia Sculptors   149
Glossary   163
Bibliography   179
Index   185
About the Author and Photographer   189

Prelude

Take a journey with me to visit some of the legends and events that contributed to making Richmond such a great place to live. They are scattered about the city in bronze and other media for our discovery.

At the risk of hurting the ears of some art creators and consumers, some "business" terms are used in explaining the following "whys" and "hows" of what makes up public art monuments.

Let's start with the four legs that support and define the success and creation (and invention) of monuments and memorials or public art. Here are the first three:

> *A. A public LOCATION is required for an installation to be public art.*

> *B. A private LOCATION, land that is not owned by the city or state, with a monumental artwork that is easily visible (or unavoidable) by the passing public and that is permanent, is required for private art.*

> *C. Some LOCATIONS are defined by their monuments instead of the other way around. In Richmond, the real estate of Monument Avenue, Hollywood Cemetery and the state capitol are expected to present the city's "greater monuments" and do.*

This is where our author, Bob Layton, clearly draws the line between greater and less identified public art monuments and memorials. Note that it is more of a quantitative line than a qualitative one.

Bob has wisely noticed this *need* to collect and write about these "lesser" installations (some of which have more significant voices than the "greater" monuments). I'm going to call this need noticed by Bob a "market need."

There are less popular monument placements that are well known among Richmonders, and there are others that are practically lost, not apparent and appreciated only by the neighboring residents. Often, they are gems, overlooked in plain sight around town. Hidden with them are their historic origins as to how and why they got there in the first place. So, addressing the same kind of "market need" of which our author became aware brings us to the fourth leg that supports the invention, creation and success of a public art installation:

> *D. The MARKET NEED must exist. Public art is an exposure for the ambient culture and society which in some way enlightens, inspires or educates. If there is not a need or use for this exposure, or if it is just one person's need or a desire by an organization, then the funding, the acquisition of a site and the social acceptance will be damaged or will fail. In short, it must be a good idea that fills or creates a genuine need.*

Inventions are like this. Consider the zipper or the indoor flush toilet. We didn't know that we needed them until they were made (publicly) available. Some public art will similarly never be let go. For example, will Paris let the Eiffel Tower fail? Will New York give up the Statue of Liberty? Both will be renewed indefinitely.

Sometimes this need is commonly recognized, perhaps to acknowledge a hero or late celebrity. At other times, the need is uncovered or invented by an artist or a person with a vision of the public art, and it goes completely unnoticed by all.

The Arthur Ashe statue is a good example. It was not originally conceived to be presented on Monument Avenue. I know a lot about this because I am the artist who recognized a need to acknowledge this Richmond-born and Richmond-educated international hero in his hometown. I saw it as a "crying market need." I knew that I could sculpt a monumental-scale (twelve feet) clay figure for about $800 and six months of work. I saw it as writing a biography, and as such, I required Mr. Ashe's authorization and then, once completed, his approval for the work to succeed. This was the "business plan" that he agreed to and also why he had "a message and details to be included" when he answered my inquiring letter with a phone call.

I was absolutely certain that there would be a place in Richmond for such a permanent acknowledgement to this great man. I was also certain that if Richmond failed to accept "the authorized and approved Arthur Ashe Statue," I would find funding and placement elsewhere: in New York, California, England, France, South Africa, Australia or elsewhere. But funding did come, albeit with much controversy. I expected it to be a "lesser monument" for Richmond, comparable in scale to the statues on Monument Avenue. But the funding nonprofit group called Virginia Heroes, the various city commissions and the city council decided to place the monument on its Avenue of Monuments—the first installation that was *not* Civil War related.

I call this an "undiscovered visual invention" that, once enjoyed by the public, becomes needed. This is not so unusual in the art world if you consider painters creating paintings on speculation (or authors writing books) and then taking them to the "market place" of ambient society and culture. In the world of business, this speculation happens all the time. The stakes are higher with public art because public art becomes public before it is finished. The vision instigators must, at some point, announce their intention to put forth to all who will listen or read the designed visual invention that they have planned and want to locate in public. Where it will go and what it will look like always provokes *some* controversy. If funding is not at least mostly in place, unenlightened or not, negative opinions can easily make raising more money impossible or prolonged to the point of failing the project. Perhaps you have heard about the pink aluminum mushroom monument designed by Salvador Dali that was planned for Monument Avenue? No? There is a reason for that. Yes? But what happened to it?

"Public art" and "private art" begin as private visions, gifts to the self in that the artist is passionate and compelled to make the art. In the case of most public art, the artist is commissioned by a person (or persons) with the vision; however, in this way, the latter is also an artist. In either case, this person takes what looks like a privilege and then sacrifices to proceed, with "risk" flashing like a lighthouse. The payoff in all outcomes is growth, but that is another book that might need to be written.

At this point, "public art" splits from "private art" because it must serve the public need to be a success. It has a requirement that private art does not. This requirement is also a purpose to tell about a "story," as in history, or tell about a "mark," as in a person who makes one. If a group or the visionary is hiring an artist to realize this "story" or "mark," then the best artist to hire is the one who can muster the most passionate tie to filling the need. Just like gift-giving, you want to give a gift that the recipient "needs" or at least wants.

There is a simple anatomical structure for public art that includes head, hands and feet:

- the head is the vision, the realization of the idea of the need; it is the discovery or the invention.
- the hands are the makers of the art and (somebody has to do it) the makers of the money to pay for it.
- the feet carry the artwork to the public, for scrutiny, socialization, politicization, enlightenment and/or edification. If these parts all fit, it is successful. The artwork survives long enough for someone to write about it.

This is the delight and the task at hand and foot for Bob Layton, now at the head. With benefit of some or much hindsight, he is exposing and bringing to focus the how, why and what of these off-the-beaten-path public art works, memorials and monuments that deserve attention. Ultimately assessing the beauty of these works, the value of the "story" and appreciation of the "mark" is up to us, the art consumers. Our author and visionary for this book makes this job more like a treasure hunt and less like a maze.

Paul DiPasquale, sculptor and practitioner
Paris, November 2012

Acknowledgements

It would be impossible to complete a book of this nature without the help of individuals and organizations. It goes so fast and there have been so many willing to assist, my only hope is to not overlook anyone.

The best place to start would be with Paul DiPasquale, who wrote the prelude. Paul found time to contribute while in a special program representing Virginia in Paris, giving the book an international flavor. His enthusiasm for the project set the tone for others' participation.

Phil Riggan was all over the city shooting the photos while holding a full-time job and attending classes at Virginia Commonwealth University. His in-depth knowledge of the monuments is evident through the book. One can understand why I latched on to him as a dependable partner and new friend.

Trying to locate material would be futile without the use of libraries, and to plow through the massive information wouldn't be possible without the staff of these helpful intuitions. Andrea Brown at the Glen Allen branch of the Henrico County system; Jody Koste at Tompkins-McCaw Museum; Ray Bonis at Virginia Commonwealth University; Cathy Wright, curator at the Museum of the Confederacy; Michelle Hevron at the Margaret R. and Robert M. Freeman Library at the Virginia Museum of Fine Arts; and Lisa Williams at Virginia Historic Resources all pitched in, as did the pleasant staff at the main Richmond Library and their remarkable clip file.

Few books of this nature ever hit the shelves without the guidance of Megan Hughes and Bill Martin at the Valentine Museum. Larry Miller at the Richmond Department of Parks, Recreation and Community Facilities showed particular interest in our project and shared important information.

Banks Smither at The History Press was valuable in guiding the process, always thorough and responsive.

Until you attempt writing a book, you can't imagine how important it is to have the support of your family. My wife, Judy, gave constant encouragement, spent many hours listening to the progress (or lack thereof) and plowed over the text with helpful recommendations. My son, Mike, also lent his intellect, making important editing changes. Both contributed without complaint, and I am lucky to have had their collaboration.

The process was not complete until the carefully trained eye of editor Ryan Finn at The History Press came to the rescue. The final product was greatly enhanced by his professional observations and recommendations.

Introduction

The early settlers didn't take long to find and claim the choice spot on the James River that we now know as Richmond. Christopher Newport and his companions came up the river and staked a cross claiming the spot short of the falls in the name of King James less than ten days after arriving in Jamestown in 1607.

Years passed before an official community was recognized. Since it was established, it has demonstrated a resilient record of survival. Fire, storm, flood, earthquake and war have all given in to the tenacity of those who call Richmond their home.

The canal system played a major role in the development of the city, providing a means of transportation for goods of the flour mills and sawmills that sprung up early and the tobacco interest that later became so important to the colonial economy. The city continued to grow and reached status to become known as "the Wall Street of the Confederacy."

This heralded past is reflected in the many monuments, memorials and statues in the city. Few cities can boast of displaying more than 150 such honors. Richmond's 1 percent allocated to arts on new construction (see Appendix III) demonstrates the dedication to acknowledge and preserve its history. Having the number one–ranked college sculpture department (Virginia Commonwealth University) in the city has also had an important impact.

The capitol building and grounds present a pantheon of statuary, busts and paintings depicting the great struggles and accomplishments of Richmond and its leaders. Hollywood Cemetery holds the resting place of notable citizens, including three presidents (four if you include Jefferson Davis). Many others have distinctive markers, statues and tombs that make this such a revered place in the city's history.

The procession of Civil War heroes on Monument Avenue, interrupted by the addition honoring Arthur Ashe, has established itself as one of the world's premier boulevards. Buildings of distinctive architecture—framed with a beautiful array of gardens and trees, graced by multiple churches and accented by cannons and generals on horseback—have caused many to describe the thoroughfare as "one of the most beautiful streets in the world." Through the years, this magnificent boulevard has seen a shifting interpretation of the South's past gain worldwide recognition.

Each of the sites just mentioned has enjoyed its share of recognition and will not be a part of this coverage. Throughout the city where Patrick Henry gave his famous "Give me liberty or give me death" speech, where Jefferson Davis set up his headquarters as president of the Confederacy and where Abraham Lincoln walked the streets after the city was burned during the Civil War, Richmond pays homage to its heroes (military, political and civic) and to its important historical events. Many among these tributes remain undiscovered and left wanting for acknowledgement.

This book seeks to remedy that void. It explores locations less visited to uncover more of the stories that have an important say about the city's history and enhance the landscape at buildings, parks and avenues. Photographs and verbiage give credence to the unsung heroes. It is hoped that this discovery will result in a better understanding of the city's history for Virginians and visitors alike and will provide a motivation for the preservation of these gems.

The entries expand on the important people and occurrences that moved Richmond in stages from a tiny burg to an important contributor to manufacturing, the arts and finance. The change in race relations and advancement in the arts is also experienced through this memorial museum. Experience the changing styles, tastes, achievements, influences and public patronage over more than two centuries. In total, the mix of the staging matches the diversity of the citizenry today.

No attempt has been made to evaluate the structures. The aim of this volume is to present a historical account of the sculptures themselves—adding anecdotal information about the person or event memorialized—rather than an artistic survey. The goal is best summed up by the inscription on the allegorical statue *Hermitage* by James Earle Fraser at the National Archives in Washington: "The Heritage of the Past Is the Seed that Brings Forth the Harvest of the Future."

Monuments are not about death; they are wholly about life. Rooted in the Latin word *monere*, meaning "to remind or admonish," monuments are not necessarily about remembering either. More often than not, they allow us to forget. Much like filing away a paper in a cabinet, erecting a monument can reinforce the slim illusion that the memories associated with it can be retrieved when desired at some later date. The very process of deciding how an event should be remembered allows us the reconciliation to move forward. Ultimately, monuments are about resolution, the outward sign that finally something has been said and done.

There is more than a passive, collective need to remember, revisit and delineate the dreams of history. The best memorials are not mere relics but rather are extraordinarily rich communications from the past, living history books that illuminate societal, political and cultural values at specific moments in time.

The difference between a monument and a memorial sees considerable debate. The former is more closely associated with large-scale civic works that celebrate a triumphalist history, while the latter speaks to commemorations that are interwoven with death and loss. Since both types mark resolution—and don't speak exclusively of death, life, triumph or loss but rather proffer a message that combines all these elements, overlaid with the element of time—both terms are used interchangeably, as are "statue" and "sculpture," along with a few that stretch such definitions.

Building monuments can be political, since what is selected to be preserved tells us everything about what is valued by the majority of the population at a given moment in history. Today, public sentiment is shaped to appreciate the more technological forms. Memorials are only built if the public, abetted by the media, places importance on a given happening, a historical figure or a leading citizen (see Paul DiPasquale's comments in the prelude).

The process of bringing an idea for a monument to completion is clouded by participation of so many from different disciplines and areas of responsibility. Politicians, administrators, community and business leaders, architects, artists, landscape architects, planners, museum personnel, arts administrators and a wide spectrum of others with interests in community development, promotion of the arts or environmental enhancement all want input. Further complication comes from the number of choices of style and construction material.

Achieving a consensus is becoming increasingly difficult as the prerequisite for public moralization (a shared set of values) is waning—if it any longer exists. In response to the need to publicly address this growing divergent understanding of history and ways of private remembrance, commemoration design often finds it hard obtaining a harmony to inspire and console.

New sculptures continue to be erected and old ones relocated. Today, that is often accomplished without fanfare in a comparatively quiet fashion. In early Richmond, the dedication of a statue often resulted in the closing of all business; crowds of twenty thousand or more attended band concerts, parades and marathon speeches that accompanied nineteenth-century dedications. Modern placements rarely command that kind of support.

Even as the obstacles are overcome and acknowledgements grace their individual positions, monuments are threatened by decay under the constant attacks of rain, air pollution, temperature fluctuation and vandalism. Polluted air produced by the burning of fossil fuels and motor vehicle exhaust eats away inscriptions and carved designs, reducing a hard, sound, outdoor sculpture into a crumbling, flaking mass within a few decades.

Recent chemical research has made it possible to arrest the decay of outdoor sculptures. A chemical can be sprayed on stone to seal the pores of the surface and to preserve the original color, texture and appearance; it also helps preserve bronze sculptures.

Richmond's outdoor museum in these forms needs ongoing vigilance to maintain the status of making history visible. Make your voice heard for the preservation of the represented heritage and use your right to be heard to nominate other tributes to be considered in the future (see Appendix IV for some ideas). In the meantime, enjoy our discoveries.

CHAPTER 1

Downtown

The diversity of the statuary in Richmond would be the envy of any city. Through the years, Richmond has paid homage to the individuals and events that contributed to the city's development. Outside the capitol grounds and away from Monument Avenue or Hollywood Cemetery, several tributes appear, telling the stories of slavery, trailblazing citizens, important events and, yes, a few additional Civil War reminders. Nowhere is this more evident than downtown, where the journey through history begins.

FIRST CROSS

Discovery starts with discovery. It occurred when Christopher Newport, John Smith, Gabriel Archer and the Honorable George Percy—with gentlemen, mariners and soldiers numbering twenty-one—explored the James River to the falls in Richmond. On Whitsunday, May 24, 1607, they knelt, prayed and erected a wooden cross with the inscription "Jacobus Rex, 1607," claiming the land for King James 1.

According to research by the Valentine Richmond History Center, the original site was near the Fourteenth Street Bridge, perhaps in the area of the Southern Railway freight depot. Three hundred years later, on the anniversary of the placement, the Association for Preservation of Antiquities

gave the city a replacement cross in copper, erected on riverbed boulders from the James River and naming the explorers mentioned on the cross placed at Gambles Hill just above Tredegar Iron Works.

In 1983, when its site was acquired by industry (actually a trade with Ethyl Corporation), the Preservation Association relocated the cross to a position in a parking lot behind the Martin Agency in Shockoe Slip.

In what may be the last move of the traveling cross, since 2003 it can be found on the Canal Walk at Twelfth Street and Byrd Avenue behind the Alcoa Building. This position is closer to its original location and more accessible for public enjoyment. It appropriately joins other entries on the Canal Walk, which stretches 1.25 miles along the historic Haxall Canal and the James River. The area does not yet rival San Antonio's River Walk, but several important historical depictions along the canal (which was begun in 1785) are worthy of note.

WASHINGTON'S VISION

Just west of the intersection of Fourteenth and Dock Streets on the canal, we find Washington's Vision, a monument dedicated in 2001. Our first president and great general was also an accomplished surveyor. He sought to connect the Atlantic Ocean to the Mississippi River with navigable rivers, canals and a land portage through what is now West Virginia.

After the Revolution, the James River Company was created, primarily as a result of Washington's sponsorship and lobbying efforts. It took nearly seventy years and the backbreaking effort of thousands

of laborers to complete the monumental task.

Before Washington's death in 1799, a large portion of his dream had been realized. Two canals bypassed the falls of the James River at Richmond to allow travel westward. This was an important contribution to the city's rise as the industrial center of the South, serving as the central link between farms and industries in the West and markets in the East, in Europe and elsewhere around the world.

By the 1820s, the Kanawha Turnpike had joined the headwaters of the James River to the Kanawha River. By 1835, the canal system had stretched to Buchanan, Virginia, a distance of 197 miles.

James Center

The story continues at the James Center (Ninth and Cary Streets). The property with its high-rise office buildings and other commercial ventures rests on what originally served as the turning basin of the Kanawha Canal during the eighteenth and nineteenth centuries, when the river was the primary mode of transportation for manufactured goods and produce. At the time, Richmond was an important industrial center and a major market for the entire area.

As a testimony to the vigorous activity of the basin, the remains of sixty-three vessels were excavated during the 1980s construction of the present-day buildings. Two iron-hulled packets, one Civil War–era rowboat, six canal freight boats and forty-eight bateaux were recovered. Portions of the original canal still remain behind the Civil War Visitor Center at the Tredegar Iron Works (500 Tredegar Street), and the entirety of the Haxall Canal has been restored. Tredegar has a significant history of its own. Founded in 1836, it made the greater part of the cannons and projectiles in the Southern states and the wrought-iron armor of the frigate *Merrimack-Virginia.*

The pedestrian walk along the restored canals includes historical markers, outdoor exhibits and public art that animate the commercial space, telling the story of yesterday. The walk provides a sense of physical direction through the James Center and gives both the everyday user and the casual visitor a sense of cultural orientation to the ancient landscape. In the words of the German poet Rainer Maria Rilke, the presentation seeks to release the "stored humanity" of the place.

Winds Up

Since November 1986, *Winds Up,* an enormous composition by Lloyd Little, has dominated the corner of Ninth and Cary Streets. The fifty-foot bronze mast with bronze sails atop a brick and stone deck designed by Alexandra Kasubabeen has three eight-foot bronze figures. The flex and curl of their muscular bodies expresses a vital energy—a sense of purpose—as they strain

while pulling halyards to hoist the sails into position. The first has just begun to pull, the second has his sail halfway up and a third has pulled his sail all the way to the top of the mast. Is it three different men laboring, or is it three different views of one man?

CORPORATE PRESENCE

Corporate Presence adds a different look to the entrance here at Ninth and Cary Streets. Completed by David Phillips and dedicated on May 13, 1985, the simple presentation shows a bronze briefcase, a calculator and a hat, each molded in a different colored patina and resting on the brick wall. The piece gives credence to the contribution of businessmen of the city who work there today. The trompe l'oeil sculpture has been very popular. Some say that from a distance they thought they had found a cache left behind by an absent-minded businessman.

BOATSMAN TOWER

Nearby, the *Boatsman Tower*, a forty-five-foot structure, watches over the activity. Crafted by Koninkiijke Eijsbouts in Asten, Netherlands, it took on this role one year after *Winds Up* was placed. The twenty-five-foot bell carillon, with cast figures representing bargemen and mules, rotates on the half hour to the tune of changing melodies. As the bells chime, cast figures of canal bargemen sing as they rotate, tilling a rudder.

The clock tower is popular with visitors as well as the Richmond workforce. It is a moving reminder of canal life and this great turning basin.

James

The curves of the James River as it twists through Richmond are traced in this bronze totem entitled *James*. The impressive bronze sculpture, standing fifteen feet high, appears in the lobby of One James Center at Ninth and Cary Streets. Once seen, the piece created by Greg LeFevre commands immediate attention, though many people are unaware that this imposing work of art is an accurate depiction of the James River as it flows through Richmond.

The polished sections of the sculpture represent the river's contours. The earth-colored textured sides suggest the surrounding curves and elements of the river's eroded banks and shallows. The artist has included a few small, almost hidden, surprise details as well. These include things one might find along the edges of the river: small fish, twigs, crayfish and the like. It is but one of LeFevre's creations that help us appreciate the importance of the James River and Kanawha Canal during this early period.

James River Divide

LeFevre is also responsible for the companion piece, *James River Divide*. Look for these six bronze panels representing different sections of the James in the same lobby where you'll also find the bank's art gallery.

The panels feature the same stretch of the river as the *James* totem but in a very different format. Using varying textures, lines, patinas and surfaces, each panel represents a different section of the river that borders downtown Richmond. The highly polished area represents the river, the corrugated bronze depicts the islands and the patina colors represent the land.

THE TURNING BASIN

LeFevre chose the floor of the James River Atrium inside the Omni Hotel for his third rendition. From an 1857 lithograph, he depicted the flow of the James River and Kanawha Canal as they move in and out of the basin using the Richmond street grid of 1813 as a guide. His work includes details of the canal locks, as well as the famous sculptures along the Capitol Square walk.

A plaque beside the map tells the story in these words:

The James Center sits in the site of the great tidal basin of the James River and Kanawha Canal. Here river packets and bateau loaded and unloaded their cargoes of tobacco, grain, iron ore, and coal from much of Virginia for local manufacturers and for destinations to the nation and to return to their port of origin. A variety of canal boats were unearthed during excavations for the James Center.

This embedded relief was abstracted from the F.N. Bears 1876 Lithographic map of Richmond and was executed by Greg LeFevre.

Also in the plaza, old stones of the Kanawha Canal are deployed in retaining walls and seating arrangements. The quality of these old stones fascinated the Virginia-born sculptor James Sanborn, who first examined the giant stone blocks where they were neatly stored under the Manchester Street Bridge, and he crafted this stone amphitheater. Others of these giant granite blocks have been arranged to suggest the outline of a typical lock on the Canal and James River. Under the careful supervision of Richmond historian Dale Wiley, and with the cooperation of the Richmond Metropolitan Authority, which lent the stones as a public service, the blocks were placed as symbols, indicating the shape, size and workings of the old locks.

WIND CHIMES

The Riverfront Plaza at Tenth and Byrd Streets hosts a bronze and granite sculptured arch by Barry Timslvey. The display is ever evolving, with the plaza located in front of the Federal Reserve building on Byrd between Eighth and Ninth Streets. A giant, unnamed wind chime of fifty-five copper rods, with patina of steel or silicon bronze, sits on a granite base. Designed by Harry Bertoia, it was placed at the elliptical pool at this address by Minoru Yamasaki.

While viewing this sculpture, take time to enjoy the attractive patio area that overlooks the riverfront. It's a good idea to browse the lobby for revolving art exhibits as well.

HEADMAN

Another water piece is found along the Canal Walk. The current *Headman*, another of sculptor Paul DiPasquale's outstanding statues, was dedicated in November 1993. It is interesting to note that there was an earlier fiberglass statue here, dedicated in May 1988.

Completion of the original fiberglass version wasn't easy. When DiPasquale contacted a Connecticut foundry about the possibility of bronzing the statue, the estimated price tag of $40,000 was nixed by the sculptor. However, further negotiation reduced the amount to $25,000, enabling him to move forward.

One year after finding a home, the original nine-foot sculpture was kidnapped. Several weeks later, *Headman* turned up in a quarry off state Route 742 in Hanover County. The statue resembled fiberglass Swiss cheese. More than four hundred bullet holes riddled its body.

Speculation spread. Some maintained that the kidnapping was racially motivated since the statue depicts a black bateau man and was erected in honor of black contributions to commerce on the James. Still others cast off the kidnapping and subsequent shooting as small-brained vandalism.

More questions were created than answered. No suspects were ever found, and *Headman* was taken back to DiPasquale's Fulton Hill studio. After more than a year of statuesque limbo, when no funds were forthcoming and when it seemed that *Headman* might disappear forever, the public took charge of its public art. Several folks called the city and complained, while others called DiPasquale and voiced support that led to the happy ending.

The replacement boat is of cypress and oak. A nine-and-a-half-foot bronze figure stands with his hands attached to a wooden oar. The returned bateau man is positioned near the foot of the bridge over the Haxall Canal at Seventh Street and has enjoyed a peaceful existence at this location.

MILL

Upstream, we find a sculpture by Bradley Robinson, a Richmond artist and blacksmith. His sculpture *Mill* has been added to the landing at the end of the bridge to Brown's Island. The two-piece, sixteen- by four-foot, brushed aluminum structure with bronze edging has a crescent-shaped bench to complement its height.

The twisted forms resemble a pair of propellers set on end. The combination is placed on direct axis with the new bridge crossing to Brown's Island to create a small and informal piazza—a place to meet or just rest.

Discussing the statue, Robinson said:

> *When designing the sculpture and benches, I was trying to maintain a tension with both the past and the present of Richmond. The piece was situated facing a very modern city, yet one could turn around and be*

enveloped by a wild river that bore the remnants of an earlier industrial age. In the final design, I chose to reference the island's industrial past but used a material (aluminum) that would relate to the contemporary buildings just across the canal. I also incorporated large granite boulders to acknowledge the natural setting of the island and its role in powering the mill that once stood there. I wanted to create a simple, elegant form that harmonizes with the surrounding beauty, both natural and architectural. I hoped to create a "place" where people could meet and interact. I wanted to honor all the men and women who labored on and around Brown's Island, particularly those who worked in the paper mill, which this sculpture directly references.

Brown's Island has a varied background. It is named for Elijah Brown, who acquired it in 1826. The first Brown's Island was created when the Haxall Canal was extended west to the Tredegar Iron Works. Encircled by the waterways that provided power and transportation to flour mills, foundries and paper companies, Brown's Island has been at the center of Richmond's industrial activities for more than two hundred years.

Remains of Civil War–era bridges can be seen from its shores, and evidence of the island once serving as a prison is still apparent.

Deepwater Sponger

Water is also the subject of one of the city's newest structures—this time it's conservation. Placed with stunning views at Rockett's Landing, *Deepwater Sponger*, by Charles Ponticello, offers a continuous reminder that quality of water for our community—and the world at large, for that matter—is essential.

Sponger, a six-foot, 1,500-pound cast-iron structure using foam and resin bonded sand moulding, depicts a hypothetical future when our water resources have drastically dwindled. Since November 2010, he has stood at this location on concrete blocks bearing the inscription, "No Water, No Life."

This presentation is part of a series begun in Baltimore by Ponticello. He plans to install others worldwide to inspire discussion and generate awareness of the state of our diminishing resource. *Sponger* serves as a catalyst for making us aware of the need for conservation and as an important reminder that only 1 percent of the planet's fresh water is available for human use, and the supply is diminishing.

Charles S. Morgan Fountain

In the popular Shockoe Slip area, where Italianate-style brick- and iron-front buildings create a European flavor in contrast with the cluster of tall modern bank buildings to the immediate west, another use of water is featured. In the center of the plaza stands an ornate fountain with an urn-type design in the Italian Renaissance style. Four gargoyle heads represent the points of the compass. The octagonal base in solid stone was placed in 1905.

The original purpose of the fountain was to supply water for the teams of horses that once hauled goods through the area. Charles S. Morgan donated the fountain, whose inscription on one side reads:

"In memory of one who loved animals."

Since 1992, the fountain has been the focal point for the "Blessing of the Animals," held on the second Friday in December. The event is intentionally brief (about thirty minutes) and is held at a time when people can participate during their lunch hour. Local businessmen are encouraged to make it a pet-friendly day at the office. As the surrounding area has become revitalized and fashionable for retail and entertainment, the popularity of the program has grown.

BOJANGLES AND FOUNTAIN

Bojangles as an entry of discovery may be inappropriate, but it is included to highlight the often-overlooked fountain directly behind this popular dancing man. This is another of the city's animal fountains. The inscription gives the history:

1908
Presented by
the National
Human Alliance

Herman Lee Ensign
founder

Few take the time to review the information on the statue. Below the dancing figure reads:

BILL
"BOJANGLES"
ROBINSON
December 14, 1878–November 25, 1949
Dancer   Author   Humanitarian
Native son of Richmond

One of the plaques reads:

Internationally famous
Actor and Dancer
Revered name
Kindness to the
Citizens of Richmond

The statue also has information relating that Reynolds Metal Company contributed the aluminum for the dancing figure and that it was sponsored by the Astoria Beneficial Club and dedicated by the citizens of Richmond and Robinson's friends throughout the world.

Before we concentrate on dry statues, we note the cascading water in the Slavery Reconciliation Statue *Triangle* and two other significant fountains at Byrd Park. For discussion of these offerings, see the Columbus statue and the Temperance Fountain in the "Parks" chapter.

Main Street offers some of the more modern contributions to the city's monuments.

QUADRATURE

Quadrature located at Tenth and Main Streets at the southwest corner of the intersection in front of the Bank of America is part of the team. Sculpted by Robert Engman, the four-piece assemblage standing twenty feet high by eight feet in diameter has stood at this position since its placement on August 9, 1985. Stainless steel cylinders set in an undulating fashion at different heights and colored blue with epoxy are said to represent the James River. Mentally piecing it together is one of the visual appeals of the work.

Future

The Twelfth Street Plaza on Main Street features James Rosati's three-legged (tripodal) aluminum sculpture entitled *Future*. Rosati is known for his work with shapes. Painted in red, this acrylic lacquer presentation stands eighteen feet high and twenty-eight feet wide and sits on a four-inch concrete base. The statue turns into an optical illusion from different angles.

Theories vary on what, if anything, the abstract work represents, but most find it interesting nonetheless. The intent was for the hard-edged diagonal aluminum abstract geometric design on three legs to symbolize control of time. Certainly it has served for a long time. It was dedicated in 1974.

Viktoria's Station

Even before it was built, Main Street Station was the darling of the city. The *Richmond Times* published the notice of the plans for a new station to serve the Chesapeake and Ohio and Seaboard Railroads in 1899. It predicted that the new depot would be "one of the greatest improvements to Richmond

in years." It continued with an advance description, noting that it was "modern in every appointment, of the handsomest stations in the country."

Main Street Station was completed in 1901 and went on to fulfill the expressed expectation. Through the years, the station has been the equivalent of a commercial citizen representing all the hardships the city has endured. The building has survived fire, storm, flood and failed retail marketing to remain one of the premier structures in the city.

The banister on the first landing of the east stairs displays a bronze ball representing the world. A depiction of a railroad track encircles the globe. The ball rests on a large slab holding a bed of railroad spikes around the ball. The inscription gets us started on explaining the honor:

VIKTORIA'S STATION

A TRIBUTE TO
THE CITY OF RICHMOND
AND
VIKTORIA BADGER
FOR
PERSEVERANCE AND VISION

C ENSLER ARCHITECTS

2003

Ms. Badger was responsible for raising more than $70,000 for the most recent renovation of the station. In addition to viewing the honor, Ms.

Badger was on hand to add to the pleasure. She explained that the design came about because in the early years of the station, a pink marble slab on which rested a marble ball anchored by four marble scroll feet sat at this location. The current whereabouts of that ball are unknown, although Ms. Badger pointed out two warped areas in the marble floor on either side of the banister where the ball once resided. She explained that passengers stood there and rubbed the ball on their way to the train level of the station. She compared the gesture to a "Godspeed rub," commenting how hundreds of thousands passed that way and so many were on their way to war. A good story and a delightful lady.

SKYRIDER

Not necessarily one of the most popular statues, *Skyrider* appears outside the Main Street Station. The creation of John Newman, it was dedicated in 2003. A hanging mixed-media sculpture, the cast-aluminum piece was commissioned by the city's Public Arts Commission. It is perched over the

station's plaza and parking lot. Interstate 95 rolls over it, creating an inversion of the normal automobile and flight vehicles.

Skyrider has survived its share of criticism. The *Richmond Times Dispatch* received twenty-two comments on the placement; nineteen criticized the piece itself. Most objected to it not having a connection to Main Street Station.

The creation is suspended in front of the station from cables beneath the canopy of overhead train tracks and expressway. Like a tightrope walker, it appears balanced high in the air as it floats over the site. The piece can be seen from all approaches to the station, as well as from passing cars and trains.

Fabricated in painted aluminum and stainless steel cable, *Skyrider* weighs in at 2,200 pounds and measures twenty-two feet high, twenty-two feet wide and fifteen feet deep. The sculptor, who worked on the project for two years, claimed that it was so complicated that he didn't make money from the effort. For better or worse, the $250,000 structure placed in 2003 excites a wide range of sensibilities.

Richmond Slavery Reconciliation Statue: *Triangle*

Our discovery takes us to remembrances of a subject most of us would like to forget, but it can't be overlooked. Though not noted among the city's finest moments, Richmond was once one of America's busiest slaves centers prior to the Civil War. Hopefully, the messages conveyed in the presentations visited next will contribute to the ongoing healing process for all of their visitors.

It took the efforts of citizens on three continents to place the Richmond Slavery Reconciliation statue at Fifteenth Street and East Main Streets. The dedication of this apology for slavery, created by Stephen Broadbent, was placed on March 31, 2007. A crowd of more than five thousand witnessed the event.

The fifteen-foot sculpture stands close to the city's former slave market and takes its place as a part of Richmond's Slave Trail as a reminder of the city's role in the slave trade. Dignitaries from around the world addressed the throng, illustrating the international importance of Richmond's Shockoe Bottom, where this awful chapter took place.

Broadbent's rendition shows two people embracing in front of three large benches that triangulate the statue, with a fountain carrying captions (read

through cascading water) describing the significance of the statue. The messages identify the three regions:

The Triangle
Liverpool, England
The Benin Region of West Africa
Richmond, Virginia

During the 18ᵗʰ Century, these three places reflected one of the
Well-known triangles in the trade of enslaved Africans.
Men, woman, and children were captured in West and Central Africa
And transported from Benin and other countries. They
were chained, herded, loaded on ships built in England and
transported through the
unspeakable horrors of the Middle Passage.

They were imported and exported in Richmond, Virginia and sold
in other American cities. Their forced labor laid the economic
foundation of this nation.

The statue itself transmits more of the wicked story. It shows chains wrapped around a map of the three jurisdictions and carries the following verbiage in both French and English:

Acknowledge and forgive the past. Embrace the present. Shape a future of reconciliation.

Identical statues appear in Liverpool, England, and Benin, West Africa, to complete the ugly story of trading in human flesh. Liverpool prospered from the slave-carrying ships, and Benin prospered as the point from which the slaves were sold in exchange for goods. It is estimated that more than 300,000 slaves and their descendants were separated from their loved ones and sold "downriver." All three jurisdictions were represented on the occasion of the dedication of the Richmond acknowledgement.

HENRY "BOX" BROWN

Nearby, another depiction of the "evil practice of slavery" offers a somewhat encouraging remembrance of this era of bondage. The Underground Railroad was used to transport slaves to freedom in the North. One of the favorite stories surrounding the success of the operation revolves around a Richmond slave, Henry Brown, who worked in one of Richmond's tobacco factories.

Mr. Brown learned about this road to liberty and made arrangements for a carpenter to construct a crate large enough for his five-foot-eight, two-hundred-pound frame.

The container had small holes for breathing and was carefully marked "This side up." The box, disguised as dry goods, was addressed to an antislavery office in Philadelphia.

Brown entered the container equipped with only a pouch of water and crackers to stave off hunger. He spent the next twenty-seven hours isolated in what must have been a torturous journey. Arriving in the North brought Brown a lot of attention, as his journey was much publicized upon the revelation of his story. Brown remained upbeat and dedicated himself to the antislavery movement after his ordeal. He became a widely known abolitionist in America and abroad.

A metal reproduction of the box in which Brown escaped has been placed near the Fourteenth Street Bridge along the Canal Walk. Appropriately labeled Box Brown Plaza, the object is a constant reminder of this escape mechanism and his ordeal.

As has been proven before, one man can make a difference. Henry Brown paved the way for others to evade unimaginably harsh living conditions. Many followed in his footsteps on the way to attaining independence and equal rights.

OLIVER HILL

The bust of Oliver Hill, civil rights lawyer of *Brown v. Board of Education* fame, acknowledges another hero from the African American community. Local sculptor Paul DiPasquale completed the piece in 2000. DiPasquale produced fifteen bronze miniatures of his creation and sold them to finance the cost for the eventual Florentine bronze bust. His task may have been aided by the fact that the project coincided with Mr. Hill receiving the Presidential Medal of Freedom from President Clinton, as well as his own fondness for his subject.

"Oliver Hill is a personal hero of mine, as was Arthur Ashe," DiPasquale said in his Fulton Hill studio in Richmond. "People who've seen the bust say it almost looks as if Oliver Hill is getting ready to say something. And he did say something. He spoke up at a time when many other people wouldn't. He said he doesn't think about age. How many soon-to-be ninety-year-olds do you know continue to work every day? He was a genuine source of inspiration for anyone who met him."

The Virginia Historical Society purchased the casting of the bust for its permanent collection. The acquisition allowed for a second casting, which

was given to the City of Richmond for public display. The bust was first placed at the visitor center at Third and Marshall Streets just half a block from where Mr. Hill practiced. It has since been moved to the Black Museum on Clay Street.

An additional tribute to Hill is found in the courts building at 1600 Oliver Hill Way, named in honor of this outstanding citizen. Here, wood carvings qualify as a memorial to his accomplishments (see the "Law Enforcement" chapter for explanation). His importance in the civil rights movement is further acknowledged in the Civil Rights Memorial at the Virginia capitol.

RIVER OF TEARS

The history of any city includes some sorrow, and Richmond is no certainly no exception. Several of the struggles that caused this are remembered in a moving presentation inside the Marshall Street entrance of Richmond's city hall. *River of Tears* is a solemn female figure draped in a robe, dedicated to victims of urban violence and their surviving family members. She represents all the tears of grief that have been shed in Richmond. More than a dozen family members of murder victims were among the nearly 150 who attended the dedication ceremony.

Linda Jordan, whose son was shot to death in front of their south Richmond home, is responsible for encouraging the sculptor to create the piece after persuading Virginia Commonwealth University to donate the time and expertise to cast the statue in bronze and after receiving permission from the city council to put the finished product in city hall.

The two-foot statue was designed by artist Donald Earley. The piece was to be the only sculpture by Earley in bronze. For his interesting career, see the "Virginia Sculptors" appendix section.

The theme of the statue was extraordinarily depicted before being placed in city hall. The statue was stolen shortly after being positioned, whereupon the city council authorized a replacement. Surprisingly, the original was returned before the substitute was completed in 1996.

While visiting city hall, pay attention to the marble walls, as they contain fossils.

VIRGINIA MOURNING HER DEAD

Some say that the best work Moses Ezekiel created was his *Virginia Mourning Her Dead*. The original statue stands proudly at the parade grounds at Virginia Military Institute, where Ezekiel was the first Jewish cadet to graduate as a member of the class of 1866.

The statue, dedicated in 1903, was moved to its present location in 1912. A female figure, representing Virginia, is shown mourning atop the remains of a fortress. Her right foot rests on broken cannons overgrown with ivy, and her right knee is raised, propping up her right elbow, which in turn holds up her head. She holds a reversed lance in her left hand, wears chain mail and sits on a piece of breastwork. Her bowed head is covered by a liberty cap.

Ezekiel crafted the piece to honor ten cadets from the school who fought and died after being wounded on the battlefield near New Market, Virginia, on May 15, 1864. Individual grave markers for the fallen cadets are visible behind the base of the sculpture. Remains of six of the young men who died are set in a copper box inside the foundation of the monument; the other four cadets are not buried at Virginia Military Institute.

This event is remembered every year on the anniversary of the battle. The name of each fallen cadet is called out; after the name, a cadet

chosen for the ceremony replies, "Died on the field of honor." Floral tributes, a prayer and a three-volley gun salute are then followed by a rendition of taps and the hymn "Amazing Grace."

Ezekiel constructed a miniature replica of the statue, and it sits proudly in the reception area (behind the gift shop) of the White House of the Confederacy at 1201 East Clay Street.

REMEMBRANCE
("RACHEL CRYING FOR HER CHILDREN")

A major interfaith gesture, believed to be the first of its kind, is responsible for one of the most moving statues in the city. Officially known as *Remembrance*, the statue is often referred to as "Rachel Crying for Her Children."

Standing in the south lawn of the cathedral on Floyd Avenue, the stirring presentation was commissioned by Walter F. Sullivan, bishop of the Catholic Diocese of Richmond, and was completed by Virginia artist Linda Gissen.

The well-known sculptor created an emotional presentation honoring the 6 million Jews who perished during the Holocaust. Six leaping bronze tongues of flame surround a weeping woman, her face cupped in her hands in full compassion for the fallen. Ms. Gissen, who donated her time, suggested that the image represents the generations of children who were not permitted to live and create because of the Holocaust.

This presentation is one of the most heartrending in the city, but despite the accessible location, it is often overlooked.

MR. SMEDLEY

Richmond lost a longtime friend, but you won't find his name in the obituaries. *Mr. Smedley*, a London busker, stood in front of the Loews Theater (later the Carpenter Center for the Performing Arts and now Richmond Center Stage) on Grace Street for eighteen years. The nine-foot-tall figure had a constant grin and could have been nominated "chief greeter" for the downtown area. *Mr. Smedley* welcomed all who passed. But he is no longer there.

By definition, a "busker" is a person who entertains (playing music, dancing, doing magic tricks and so on) in public places. The talents of the busker run from the acoustic singer-songwriter types to didgeridooists. Although governed by rules and a code of conduct, buskers are controversial in most cities where they appear. They are often labeled "loiterers" or "noisemakers."

That was not the case in Richmond. Our busker was the quiet type. How many times have you passed *Mr. Smedley*, standing in front of his trunk of tricks at this position of high traffic? He got attention by reversing his vest and buttoning it in the back; he carried a teddy bear in his hip pocket and held a small dog in his right hand. His left hand lifted his hat as if to say hello. Those who looked closely noted that this friendly gesture revealed a mouse sitting on top of his head.

Mr. Smedley was often mistaken for the better-known statue of Bill "Bojangles" Robinson that stands at Leigh and Adams Streets. This is understandable since the same wit produced these fine pieces. Mr. John T. ("Jack") Witt, a talented local sculptor residing in Ashland, Virginia, created both.

Mr. Smedley was removed in preparation for the renovation for the new performing arts project. Reminiscent of the words of Mark Twain, who said that the reports of his death were greatly exaggerated, the good news is that the city acted to protect the statue. For the time being, *Mr. Smedley* rests in storage with the Richmond Department of Recreation and Parks. There is encouraging activity to restore the happy fellow to active duty in the near future.

WAR HORSE

Whether to include the horse that stands on the veranda of the Virginia Historical Society is debatable as a discovery, but its story is one that is often not understood.

Don't be too quick to judge the posture of what is sometimes referred to as "the horse of remorse." There is an explanation for its despondent stance. Noting the thousands of statues honoring Civil War soldiers and none existing paying tribute to equine efforts and losses, Mr. Paul Mellon commissioned the statue.

The assignment fell to noted English equestrian artist Tessa Pullan, FBRS, SEA, of Rutland, England, with whom Mellon had worked previously—the sculptor had produced a three-fourth life-size bronze of Sea Hero, Mellon's 1993 Kentucky Derby winner.

When contemplating the placement, with full appreciation of her talents, Mr. Mellon was quoted as saying, "Tessa Pullan's interpretations of animal life have a directness and honesty which mirror the alert, vital and spontaneous quality of the animals themselves. Whether untamed or domestic, whether depicted in repose or moving with grace, there is something about these enormously attractive forms which rivets the eye and warms the heart."

Further attesting to the significance of the piece, Dr. William M.S. Rasmussen of the Virginia Historical Society shared these thoughts: "This is one of the best pieces of outdoor sculpture to be introduced to the Richmond landscape since Jean-Antoine Mercie's *Lee* was unveiled a hundred years earlier. It's only a horse, but the sculpture can be viewed as more, as a symbol of the suffering inflicted on so many living creatures in Virginia during the Civil War. People from all ways of life were affected. This is a message that is very easy for us to forget today, partly because it isn't offered at all by the Monument Avenue sculptures."

The inscription on the base of the statue speaks with clarity to all who review it close up:

In Memory
Of the One and One Half Million
Horses and Mules of the Confederate
And Union Armies Who Were Killed,
Were Wounded or Died from Disease
In the Civil War

Ms. Pullan truly captured the intended mission—the magnificent steed looks its role. The veranda rendition is her third horse of this kind. The first *War Horse* was placed outside the National Sporting Museum in Middleburg, Virginia. A second statue was set at the United States Cavalry Museum in Fort Riley, Kansas. The historical society's horse was enlarged from the original's quarter-horse size to ensure proportion on the veranda.

Perhaps this background will enhance your next visit to this esteemed symbol. The historical society placement makes it possible to enjoy this work of art on a regular basis. A miniature copy is available in its gift shop on the Boulevard. It is truly a conversation piece.

To end this section on a positive note, we visit Thomas Jefferson, one of Virginia's favorite founder icons. Our third president makes several appearances in the city in a variety of poses, in addition to appearing more than once in the capitol building, including as a Jean-Antoine Houdon creation and also his location at the base of the equestrian statue of George Washington on the capitol grounds.

JEFFERSON HOTEL

Jefferson is found at the five-star Jefferson Hotel, built by tobacco entrepreneur Lewis Ginter. Edward V. Valentine, well-known Richmond sculptor, did the beautiful Carrara marble statue of the third president. Valentine was able to borrow clothing actually worn by Jefferson that he copied for the piece. He labored on the work for more than two years. It was completed in 1890.

Valentine didn't leave much to be imagined about Jefferson. The statue is loaded with information. Below Jefferson is inscribed:

Governor
of
Virginia
1779–1787

In his right hand, the inscription reveals that he holds that wonderful document that got us off to such a good start:

The original Draft of the Declaration of Independence, Passed by the Continental Congress of the United States of America, 1776.

Under the right arm, it reads:

Born at
Shadwell in the county of
Albemarle, Virginia.

April 13, 1743,
died at Monticello, Virginia
July 4, 1826.

Behind Jefferson is recorded:

Vice President of the
United States of America
1797–1801,
Third President
of the United States of America
1801–1805
1805–1809

Below the left arm the text is:

William Thomas Jefferson,
Author
of
the Declaration of Independence
and
the State of Virginia for Religious Freedom
and
Father
of
the University of Virginia.

When a fire broke out in the hotel in 1901, the statue was badly burned. The handsome piece could have been lost forever but for some quick thinking. The head of Jefferson was disengaged as a rescue team (including Valentine) carried the statue out on mattresses to safety. Fortunately, the sculptor was able to reattach it. As a result of the injury, the statue requires regular maintenance, but it has maintained its iconic nature, including serving as a backdrop for several television programs.

First placed facing south at the foot of the grand staircase, the statue has been moved to face east in the Palm Court area, once the home of the Rotunda Club but perhaps better known as the place where alligators once resided. Jefferson stands near the main entrance to the hotel to greet travelers as they arrive.

THE THOMAS JEFFERSON BUILDING

Jefferson also stands tall with dioramas illustrating his many talents—farmer, inventor, architect, writer, educator and accountant—carved in the north-facing wall of the Jefferson Building, formerly known as the Blanton Building. The outstanding presentation, placed in 1957, has been often overlooked due to its partially hidden position on Governor Street. Located just south of the Governor's Mansion, the street has been closed to vehicular traffic since 9/11.

JEFFERSON STANDING ON THE LIBERTY BELL

At the Library of Virginia (Ninth and Broad Streets), Jefferson stands above the Liberty Bell in the east corridor on the first floor. The statue is a miniature of the original by Moses Ezekiel, Richmond-born and internationally known sculptor who created the work for Jefferson County, Kentucky, in 1901. Ezekiel also made three copies.

A life-size replica is on the north side of the rotunda at the University of Virginia. Another miniature is held by Virginia Military Institute and is housed at its museum at New Market, Virginia.

Use of the Liberty Bell as a statue base was a novel idea Ezekiel had planned to use in his *Religious Liberty* monument of 1876 but later abandoned. When Isaac and Bernard Bernheim of Louisville, Kentucky, approached him to memorialize the Virginian for whom the county is named, Ezekiel outlined his plan to rejuvenate the idea in a letter to the brothers. Referring to the bell, he stated he would use an "exact copy."

Close inspection reveals that this didn't quite happen. Several inaccuracies were discovered. Throughout his heralded career, Ezekiel had accurately executed statues of historical figures, artists and poets. This was not to be one of those occasions. The liberties the sculptor took in copying the nation's symbol of freedom are difficult to understand in light of the fact that he followed some of the changes made by John Pass and John Stow, who had recast the original bell.

The combination of Jefferson and Philadelphia's famous bell was a good start for a stunning work. The statue conveys multiple messages that remain important today. Just why the sculptor decided to rearrange the bell remains unknown.

Ezekiel's rendition is a composite of twelve separate castings. Jefferson holds the Declaration of Independence as he prepares to read it to the Continental Congress. Around the base of the bell, four winged female figures representing the Jeffersonian ideas of Brotherhood, Justice, Equality and Liberty have been added. The figure of Brotherhood holds a scroll referring to Jefferson's Statute for Religious Freedom, passed in 1786, a copy of which is in the collections of the Library of Virginia. Justice is blindfolded; she holds a sword in her left hand and a balance in her right. Equality tears up the laws of primogeniture and stands on the laws that Jefferson listed as grievances with King George II and the British Parliament. Liberty thrusts her arms back and breaks the chain of bondage; like Justice, she holds a sword in her left hand.

None of these angel figures is found on our national Liberty Bell, and they serve to accent or hide other discrepancies that are distinguishable in Ezekiel's presentation:

- Pennsylvania is spelled correctly (the Liberty Bell uses "Pensylvania").
- The abbreviation of Leviticus is different.
- No portion of the Pass and Stow names were included.
- The Roman numeral date was omitted.
- The insertion of the year 1752 is incorrect (the original bell was completed in 1753).
- The words "Pennsylvania Assembly" were omitted.
- "Province" was not capitalized.

The mistakes have not marred the reputation of the statue. It is considered one of Ezekiel's most successful and has been admired by citizens of Kentucky and Virginia and thousands of visitors for more than a century.

The national bell we cherish is actually the third bell cast. The first was done in Whitechapel Foundry outside London, England, for the Pennsylvania State House. This bell famously cracked on the first attempt to ring it. Pass and Stow had the same result with their first attempt but produced a useable bell on their next effort. Every state has a copy of the bell. Virginia's can be found at a fire station in Charlottesville.

CHAPTER 2

Virginia Commonwealth University

Since 1838, the Medical College of Virginia (MCV), now a division of Virginia Commonwealth University, has been in the forefront of advances in healthcare, providing patients with some of the most progressive treatment and technology available. With more than two hundred areas of specialty, it serves more than 500,000 patients per year. The institution enrolls more than 27,000 students annually. Numerous awards attest to its expertise, but culture at MCV is more than a colony of microorganisms found in a petri dish. Many examples are found throughout the campus.

The university's School of Sculpture has traditionally rivaled the medical section for top national ranking, and the campus demonstrates its diversity with displays of a wide selection of art.

HUNTER HOLMES MCGUIRE

A few surprises await when you enter McGuire Hall, a structure housing offices, classes, training facilities and laboratories of the School of Medicine for the Departments of Occupational Therapy and Rehabilitation Counseling.

You first notice a bust of Hunter McGuire, the legendary physician who gained much of his notoriety at MCV and was largely responsible for its

growth. The sculpture sits on steps in the foyer and looks you in the eye as you enter the building from Clay Street. McGuire is worthy of the accolades registered on his statue at the capitol:

To
Hunter Holmes McGuire, M.D., L.L.D.
President of the American Medical
and of the
American Surgical Associations;
Founder of the University College of Medicine
Medical Director, Jackson's Corps,
Army of Northern Virginia.
An Eminent Civil and Military Surgeon
And Beloved Physician.
An Able Teacher and Vigorous Writer;
A Useful Citizen and Broad Humanitarian,
Gifted in Mind and Generous in Heart,
This Monument is Erected by His Many Friends.

BENJAMIN FRANKLIN

Don't let the McGuire bust distract you and cause you to miss the miniature statue of Benjamin Franklin. Franklin stands inside the chandelier, just inside the door. Perched within the fixture that was once a gasolier, he watches over all visitors whether they see him or not.

Another gasolier featuring Franklin appears one block east in the White House of the Confederacy. Taken from a New Bedford, Massachusetts home (circa 1850), it now is found in the foyer where Jefferson Davis's secretary greeted visitors. The introduction of gas lighting to Richmond in 1851 allowed Lewis Ginter to add gasoliers to his mansion.

The only other honor Benjamin Franklin earned in Richmond was to have the original F Street changed to Franklin Street when the east–west corridors were renamed.

THREE BEARS

Inside the Medical College of Virginia hospital at the main registration lobby, a stone grouping shows three small bears frolicking. Moved from its original post on the circular drive at the corner of Twelfth and Broad Streets, the statue is a gift from Archer M. and Anne Hyatt Huntington of Brook Green Garden in South Carolina. The work is a reproduction of the original at their estate.

The cubs, shown playing with twigs, symbolize the healing creeds of Native Americans. Indian medicine looks to the bear, the strongest animal on this

continent, as a source of strength and power. During times of affliction, Indians have ceremoniously offered prayer and hymns to invoke the demigod's help.

The gift is a fitting reminder of MCV's threefold responsibility: to educate those who serve humanity, to preserve and restore health and to seek the cure of diseases.

Nearby, the Egyptian Building, the South's oldest medical college structure still in use, is a classic example of the Egyptian Revival style of architecture utilized in America in the early 1800s. The edifice of the building exhibits battered walls; columns with capitals of palm leaves; and symbolic medallions, each featuring a sun disc, wings and a serpent. The fence surrounding the building is one of a kind, with posts in the form of mummies with exposed toes and simulated wrap. Another small fenced area in the round uses obelisks as posts.

HIPPOCRATES

The courtyard of the Egyptian Building contains a bust of Hippocrates, a replica of another in Athens, Greece. The piece was carved from marble taken from Penteliko Mountain near Athens. A gift from Virginians of Greek ancestry, the mounted piece was sculpted by Menelaos Katafigiostis at a cost of $20,000.

The inscription on the statue is consistent with the wisdom of Hippocrates but stretches to fields outside his medical proficiency:

Hippocrates
460–377 BC

LIFE IS SHORT ART IS LONG
OPPORTUNITY FUGITIVE
EXPERIENCE DELUSIVE
JUDGMENT DIFFICULT

[the same message is repeated in Greek]

PRESENTED AND DONATED BY VIRGINIANS OF GREEK DESCENT

ST. PHILIP HOSPITAL ARCH

The eight-foot copy has moved around the courtyard, but it now rests under the original arch entrance of Dooley Hospital. Across the courtyard, in the lobby of the Medical Sciences Building, the designers were thoughtful enough to preserve the original arch entrance to St. Philip Hospital that once occupied this location (until 1996). Established by the Medical College of Virginia in 1920, an era of racial segregation, it became an important part of the MCV history. St. Philip was the training ground for black nurses, graduating almost seven hundred during its existence, which lasted until 1962. Five years earlier, the MCV School of Nursing admitted its first African American student.

MONUMENTAL CHURCH

One of the crown jewels of Richmond architecture is not necessarily thought of as a monument. Truly marking a historical event and connecting with such notables as the Marquis de Lafayette (who worshiped there), John Marshall,

Robert Mills, Gilbert Hunt and Governor Billy Smith, Monumental Church (fronting on Broad Street) is a memorial with a significant history.

The events and individuals connected with this property are exceptional. On December 26, 1811, the theater occupying this space succumbed to a fire, which resulted in a tragedy that saw seventy-two Richmond theatergoers lose their lives. Citizens from all walks of life were in the casualty list, including then governor George W. (Billy) Smith.

Most of those lost in the fire were women and children, despite the gallant attempt of one Gilbert Hunt, a slave and blacksmith, who gained his freedom by his heroic act of catching jumping patrons.

A committee headed by Chief Justice John Marshall gathered funds to build the replacement structure that we know today. Robert Mills—of Washington Monument fame in Washington, D.C.; works in Baltimore, Maryland; and other important government buildings—won the contest for his design of the church. The memorial was completed, and the consecration took place on May 14, 1814. The sandstone Mills used was taken from Aquia Creek in northern Virginia. This same stone was used for the White House in Washington.

All care was taken to honor the deceased as Mills understood the Egyptian tradition of honoring the dead in powerful and permanent forms, and his use of Egyptian elements in the design is evidence of his admiration for the buildings of antiquity.

In the portico's center, the monument combines a sarcophagus base with a Roman-inspired urn. The names of the victims are carved into the walls of the sarcophagus, and its cavetto cornice is decorated with a winged orb, an emblem of the creation and preservation of life taken from Egyptian temples. A steeple was originally planned to top the tower at the rear of the church but was never erected.

On either side of the pulpit, columns decorated with inverted torches symbolize life snuffed out. The gallery is supported with columns topped with sarcophagus-shaped capitals and decorated with inverted torches. Lachrymatories in the frieze convey the monument's purpose as a symbol of mourning and veneration of the dead. The window heads of the church are in the shape of sarcophagi, carrying out the theme of the monument to the body of the building and to the bodies of the perished that were laid below the building.

Recent renovation makes this a showplace not to be missed; it is one of Richmond's prize possessions.

MEDICAL COLLEGE DOOR GRILL

A few paces west on the south side of the Medical College Hospital, we find a tribute to the giants of medical history. An impressive grill above the entrance carries information about those who contributed to the cure of disease and illness:

Hippocrates 450 B.C. "Father of Medicine."

Gayland Pergamun 129–199 2nd Century writer who compiled the medical treatment and effects of his day.

Andreas Vesalius 1514–1564 16th C Italian "father of anatomy."

William Harvey 1578–1657 English physician who discovered the circulatory system in 17th C.

Edward Jenner 1749–1823 English physician who developed small pox vaccination in 18th C.

Rudolph Virchow 1821–1902 German pathologist of 19th C who discovered cell structure.

Louis Pasteur 1822–1895 French chemist and bacteriologist who originated theory of disease immunity—pasteurization of milk named after him.

Joseph Lister 1827–1912 English surgeon who developed anesthetic surgery.

At the top of the door frame, "West Hospital" is spelled out, and the bottom identifies the "Medical College of Virginia Hospital."

OLD DOMINION HOSPITAL OPERATING FACILITY

On the other side of Broad Street, in the Department of Motor Vehicles Building on the southeast corner of Governor and Twelfth Streets, an original operating room is preserved on the third floor. When it was in use, it was part of the Old Dominion Hospital at that address (circa 1903). The hospital dates back to 1838. A reservation is recommended if you desire a visit. Should you be contemplating surgery, you'll be glad to learn that the replacement facilities have been upgraded.

BOY ON STILTS

Not to be outdone, the dental division of the college features *Boy on Stilts*, a statue by Dr. William H. Turner, DDS. It decorates Malborn Garden and was established in memory of Bennett A. Malborn, DDS. Turner studied at the dental school and practiced before he began his career working in porcelain, and he also went on to be an internationally recognized sculptor in bronze.

Since creating the sculpture in 1993, Turner has completed copies in three different sizes. Turner's grandson, now a graduate student, modeled for the statue, and it was given to the School of Dentistry anonymously by a woman who admired Dr. Turner's work.

The statue shows a boy walking on stilts made from tree limbs, with his dog joyfully nipping at his heels. Turner elaborated on the creation, claiming that the boy symbolizes an earlier time in our history and in his own life. "You know," he said, "back when I was growing up, you couldn't go out to the store and buy toys. We had to make them, and this piece represents that time…I grew up carving wood to make my play things." He went on to reminisce about his barefoot summer days that influenced *Boy*'s design. Turner has also written books telling stories of his rural beginning.

EUGENE P. TRANI

Perhaps there could be a more cheerful remembrance of the long-term president of Virginia Commonwealth University than the rendition in the atrium of the Eugene P. Trani Training Center for Life Services at 1000 West Cary Street. A lifelike and life-size statue done by VCU School of Arts graduate Ruby L. Westcott renders him as subdued and thoughtful as he considers his next achievement. The $60,000 required for the statue was raised through contributions.

Trani held the position of president of the university from 1990 to 2009. During his reign, he spearheaded a $1.2 billion infrastructure building program that changed the landscape of the campus and influenced major sections of Richmond. He saw the university grow from a small commuter school to a sprawling state institution and was instrumental in nationalizing the university in both the student body and the courses offered.

TRUTH AND BEAUTY

Truth and Beauty, another of Lester Van Winkle's unusual presentations, was created by him working in harmony with Ross Caudill, VCU adjunct professor of sculpture, while serving as professor emeritus. Two oversized winged desks, made of bronze and stainless steel and facing a large easel with a sketch of Henry H. Hibbs, founder of the Richmond School of Social Economy—the previous name for the Richmond Professional Institute (RPI) and VCU—were revealed on the occasion of the fortieth anniversary (2008) celebration of Virginia Commonwealth University.

Van Winkle, who taught at VCU for almost all of those forty years, said that he envisioned that the piece would invite participation by visitors. The sculpture is an homage to a classroom—a kind of "transparent classroom." The oversized desks are elevated to keep visitors' feet off the ground, eliciting a childlike feeling. Books entitled "Beauty," "Truth" and "Character" are visible on and under the desks.

"When I pictured it, I saw it with people standing in it," Van Winkle said. "Without folks wandering through, it doesn't function the way I want it to. I hope it becomes a very special locale on campus—a place where people congregate, where lovers meet, where people come and contemplate their navel. I hope it's a special kind of place where visitors feel some sense of what this place is about."

Van Winkle featured Hibbs in the piece because of an admiration for his work at RPI. "I think of Richmond as a city of wonderful ghosts, a city that all of these brilliant minds have walked through," Van Winkle said. "Hibbs is part of that, a wonderful specter whose reputation as an educator and humanist is very enviable." The placement between Hibbs Hall and Anderson Gallery in the Shafer Court area of the campus is fitting.

TABLEITH

The fortieth anniversary was the setting for another contribution, this time by a graduate who received his MFA in sculpture from VCU. Charles Ponticello presented *Tableith*, created to honor RPI and its connection to VCU. Weighing in at more than twenty tons, the piece includes fifty-one cast discs stacked atop one another and spiraling upward. Each of the discs is inscribed with historical information or key events from the years between 1917 and 1968, when RPI merged with the Medical College of Virginia to form VCU.

"My primary focus is to produce a monumental effect with a sense of awe and respect rather than a 'stand out' personal interpretation with imagery that overcomes the purpose," Ponticello said in an artist's statement accompanying the piece during a competition conducted by the RPI Sculpture Committee, which included several alumni. In a later statement, he elaborated on his objective: "I purposely designed it with the 'founders' stone leaning at its base with the two unfinished stones several feet away. My intention was to give the viewers a sense of continuing growth while adding additional seating to the environment."

Tableith is located just west of Ginter House, which was known as the Ad Building during RPI's existence. The building held a particular importance to RPI students, who gathered in front of the building as a meeting place.

William O'Connell, a member of the RPI Sculpture Committee, said that the sculpture will serve as a prominent physical reminder of RPI's legacy at VCU. "The idea was to create some lasting object that would let people know that there was a precursor to VCU," O'Connell noted. "It's a way of letting the current students know about the history of their school. It's an exciting project for the RPI graduates. It will be a very special thing to have something established on campus that will ensure that RPI is always recognized as being part of the university."

CHAPTER 3

Parks

We tend to think of parks as isolated areas of grass and trees for relaxation and recreation and as places to swim, hike and play games—in general, places to have fun. Richmonders have multiple choices to take advantage of the opportunity to be physically active, reduce stress and enhance their sense of wellness. It is important to have close-to-home access to places where one can recreate. Many authorities on the subject contend that it is a key factor linking whether or not people will lead healthy lives.

Several Richmond spaces have the serendipitous benefit of featuring cultural presentations on the same property. Richmond has a long history of offering a variety of ways to promote the understanding of its past. The following pages will assist your discovery while visiting these set-aside properties.

BYRD PARK

The first stop for a review of park culture is Byrd Park. This space got its start in 1902 as the West End Electrical Park. It began with a roller coaster and a huge swimming pool. Its name was changed to Idlewood Park upon being leased to a promoter, who built a four-thousand-seat horse show building and a casino where vaudeville and musical entertainment took place. At that time, the park also featured a baseball batting gallery, a shooting gallery, a mammoth carousel capable of handling one hundred riders and the "Circle Swing," said to give the effect of being in a boat on the "billowing Main."

The enterprise faltered when prohibitionists demonstrated their concern that bar receipts were the highest source of revenue despite the other offered delights.

Through it all, the beautifully landscaped 287-acre park remains one of the premier properties set aside for recreation. Two lakes, several tennis courts, a round meetinghouse, a children's playground, ball fields, picnic shelters and a trail provide a wide choice for exercise and enjoyment. Its proximity to Maymont Park connects it to a popular playground for all ages. No further testimony to the park is needed when one realizes that it was here where Arthur Ashe got his early training to become one of the great stars of tennis.

Columbus

Columbus may be more notable for discovering America, but a statue of the explorer standing outside one of the main entrances to Byrd Park gets a lot of traffic. A planned Columbus Day (October 12, 1927) dedication was postponed until December 8, 1927, because the Italian ambassador could not attend the earlier date. Sponsored by the Italian Citizens of Virginia, this was the first Columbus statue in the South. This is significant as it occurred before the 1934 congressional resolution declaring Columbus Day a national holiday.

Many dignitaries attended the dedication, including the Italian ambassador, carrying a message from Mussolini. The six-and-a-half-foot-tall figure stands above an eight-and-a-half-foot granite pedestal. Ferruccio Legnaioli, a prolific Richmond sculptor, created the statue. Columbus became the first illuminated statue in the city. The fountain behind the statue was added in 1938 as a project of the Public Works Administration.

It all got started when Frank Realmuto, an Italian barber who worked at the Central YMCA, started a crusade to memorialize his countryman. He obtained the support of the Italian American Society and began to raise the money to complete his idea.

Temperance Fountain

Close by, on park property near the Roundhouse, is another fountain, founded on the rhyming temperance pledge of the nineteenth-century movement:

> *To quench our thirst we'll always bring*
> *Cold water from the well or spring*
> *So here we pledge our perpetual hate*
> *To all that can intoxicate*

The inscription on the fountain confers its own history:

THIS FOUNTAIN
IS ERECTED BY THE WOMAN'S
CHRISTIAN TEMPERANCE UNION
OF RICHMOND CITY AND HENRICO COUNTY
AND THEIR FRIENDS IN MEMORY OF THE
THE CRUSADERS OF HILLSBORO, OHIO WHO
WENT OUT DECEMBER 19, 1873 WITH THE
WEAPONS OF PRAYER AND FAITH IN GOD
TO OVERTHROW THE LIQUOR TRAFFIC

AND ALSO IN MEMORY OF
FRANCES E. WILLARD
ORGANIZER OF THE WOMAN'S
CHRISTIAN TEMPERANCE UNION

The closing statement of the inscription is poetic:

THE FINEST BATTLE THAT WAS EVER FOUGHT:
SHALL I TELL YOU WHERE AND WHEN?
ON THE MAPS OF THE WORLD YOU WILL FIND IT NOT,
'TWAS FOUGHT BY THE MOTHERS OF MEN.

The May 27, 1927 dedication of the fountain was concluded prematurely by a drenching rain. The monument erected for the cause of a dry America promptly got wet!

Frances Willard continued as a leader of the temperance union and went on to become a key figure in the struggle for women's suffrage. She is one of the few women to be memorialized by a statue in Statutory Hall in our nation's capital. Willard stands tall, representing Illinois as one of two nominees allocated to each state for such an honor.

On the opposite side of the Roundhouse, grave sites for the Shields and Robinson families, who owned the property in the early years of the city, are found behind a brick wall. Nearby, both names appear on street signs honoring their contributions to the development of the city. The Robinson house, on the grounds of the Virginia Museum of Fine Arts, is still maintained and used for art instruction.

James Henry Dooley Monument

Opposite the parking lot to the Hampton Street entrance to Maymont, in a small park owned by St. Joseph's Villa, stands an elaborate pinnacle. It is a tribute to James Henry Dooley, honoring his generous philanthropic contributions.

Adopted from the Pillar Cross Sundial at Corpus Christi College in Oxford, England, the octagonal shape stands on three steps representing Faith, Hope and Charity. The pyramided pinnacle's top is decorated with a sundial, and the cross head sides bear the arms of the Catholic diocese of Richmond, the Dooley family arms, the seal of Virginia and the seal of Richmond.

A second sundial, of a different design and facing south, appears on an eight-sided stepped shaft, about twenty feet high. Directions for the use of the sundials are inscribed on the second-tier base. Instruction for the plus or minus adjustment to the sun time indicated on the dials is given by dates throughout the year.

The inscription running around the top of the third step commemorates Dooley's $3 million gifts:

> *This square and building thereupon dedicated to Charity by James H. Dooley in memory of his father Maj. John Dooley, his mother Sarah P. of his wife S. Dooley and himself.*

On top of the base, it reads:

> *This park is maintained as a perpetual memorial of his charitable bequest. James H. Dooley to be erected on the square and have by decree of court*

located at Hollybrook on the Washington Highway about three miles north of Richmond.

The statue has a variety of symbols, including shields featuring animals (cow, lion, ram and eagle), tributes to several saints, leg cuffs, a cress, a pitcher and cup, a knife cutting bread, a casket and shovel and a church with its entrance door open. Grapes, vines and a fruit basket with flowers round out the visual language of the presentation.

Dooley, one of the founders of Seaboard Railroad, built and financed the Cripple Children's Hospital, St. Joseph's Villa, Dooley Hospital at MCV-VCU and Maymont, the Dooley residence. Richmond Main Public Library was a bequest from Mrs. Dooley's estate.

Maymont

Maymont is a popular family attraction, offering a variety of activities, including a museum, formal gardens, native wildlife exhibits, a nature center, gardens, a carriage collection and a children's farm. The Dooley mansion sits above the James River in a picturesque setting.

Bear Monument

At one time, the Children's Farm and Wildlife Exhibits on these beautiful grounds included a den of bears. A bizarre biting incident ended in citizen outcry to the extent that the bears were euthanized. But that was not the end of the story.

A strong contingency had always enjoyed visiting the bears and felt that the reaction, caused by the actions of one aggressive child, was too drastic. More than five hundred attended the funeral for "Buster" and "Baby." Charles and Sibyl Thalhimer were so moved that they donated a large bear statue for the grounds in 2006. The figure was created by William Turner, internationally known Virginian sculptor. The statue is found in an area across from the original bear habitat. (Although not a part of this presentation, some may be interested to know that inside the Dooley mansion, more than one hundred animals appear on dinnerware, furniture carvings and statuary.)

Three Graces

On the lawn of the Dooley mansion's exquisite property is a copy of artist Antonio Canova's *Three Graces*. Faithful to Neoclassical ideas, Canova embodied his perceptions of beauty in the form of ancient goddesses who were said to personify feminine charm.

Dedicated in the late 1800s, the three marble female figures overlook the James River, standing approximately five and a half feet tall on a two-foot base and representing Splendor, Mirth and Good Cheer. The figures are carved in the Roman tradition, intertwined with garlands, ribbons and drapery.

Contemporaries praised the work for its new approach to the subject. Unlike compositions that derived from antiquity—where the outer figures turn out toward the viewer and the central figure embraces her friends with her back to us—Canova's figures stand side by side, all facing one another.

The three female figures become one in their embrace, united not simply by their joined hands but also by the scarf that drops from one of their hands. Canova's composition is so compact and balanced that many have declared the statue "more beautiful than beauty itself."

Follow the Leader (Children at Play)

Follow the Leader (*Children at Play*), a statue of children and a dog romping on a sculpted log, is also found on the grounds. The piece, provided by an anonymous donor, is located near the children's farm at the end of the parking lot from the Spotswood entrance to the park. It was composed by W. Stanley Proctor, who has placed the same statue at the governor's mansions in Florida; in Sedona, Arizona; and in Ludington, Michigan. The sculptor also executed a similar design for a Summerville, South Carolina installation.

Stop by on any sunny day, and you will find children playing on the statue. Keep a close watch, as the statue is so realistic that you may have difficulty distinguishing which of the children are yours.

Relaxing at Shields Lake

Close by, another tree presentation hasn't made it. Two wooden logs representing relaxing people were laid on a hill above Shields Lake. Labeled, appropriately, *Relaxing at Shields Lake*, it was made with logs from the Richmond Department of Parks and Recreation. It was given by an anonymous donor and done by a local artist, James Michael "Mike" Marr.

Mr. Marr was proud of the fact that he was able to place a statue in Richmond without controversy, relating to the debate over placing the Arthur Ashe statue on Monument Avenue and the mural of Robert E. Lee on the floodwall. He speculated that his success was influenced by the fact that you cannot determine the genders of his "people."

At last word, the statue had become weather beaten and insect infected and may be beyond repair. We can only hope for the recovery of these characters so they can return to set the example for leisure at the lake.

Sam Woods Memorial

Before leaving Byrd Park, see the Sam Woods memorial plaque, honoring a man who made a major contribution to the youth of the city. The honor is located at the south end of the tennis courts. The inscription explains:

> *Sam Woods Memorial*
> *Tennis Court*
> *In Memory of*
> *Sam Baker Woods*
> *1892–1963*

For more than a score of years (1943–1963) no citizen contributed more to the wholesome development of youth of Richmond than Sam Woods.

On these courts he endeared himself and earned lasting obligation From all who came within his influence. From his endeavors emerged many of the state's outstanding players as well as eleven state championship teams from Thomas Jefferson High School. His interest in tennis was not confined to the making of champions but was directed to developing high qualities of sportsmanship, physical fitness, and character in boys and girls alike.

This plaque presented by the Richmond Tennis Patrons Association in tribute to the memory of Samuel Baker Woods whose dedication to youth and whole life of unselfish service affords an inspiration to us all.

CHIMBORAZO PARK

Since 1870, the city has operated the forty-acre plateau in the east end called Chimborazo as a park. Said to be named after the Ecuadorian volcano Mount Chimborazo, it sits high above the James River, offering several views and preserving and recording the history of this property as one of the more important stories of Civil War Richmond.

Markers tell us that the property was the largest military hospital in the world. Established by Surgeon General S.P. Moore (Confederate States of America) and directed by Dr. James B. McGuire, it consisted of 150 buildings and one hundred tents. More than seventy-six thousand patients were cared for, with a mortality rate of less than 10 percent. Today, the park houses significant archives of the city's and the county's history in the National Battlefield Park Headquarters Museum on the premises.

Statue of Liberty Replica

Near the rear of the park, a miniature version of the Statue of Liberty stands eight and a half feet tall on a sixteen-foot-wide base made of cobblestones from the streets of Richmond. The statue was given by the Richmond Robert E. Lee Council of the Boy Scouts of America as part of a nationwide program. The Strengthen the Arm of Liberty program was kicked off when scouts teamed with corporations to distribute more than two hundred copies of the monument throughout America carrying the inscription here. The campaign was kicked off with a torch-lighting ceremony beneath the Statue of Liberty in New York Harbor. Similar ceremonies were conducted coast to coast. The Cold War with the Soviet Union had just begun:

With the faith and courage of
Their forefathers who made
possible the freedom of these
United States

*The Boy Scouts of America
dedicated this copy of the
Statue of Liberty as a pledge
of everlasting fidelity and
loyalty
40th anniversary crusade to
strengthen the arm of liberty
1950*

The Richmond copy arrived in January 1951. Over the years, the replica has experienced some vandalism, but as of this writing, it is in good repair, as are many others across the land.

Powhatan Stone

Close by the Powhatan Stone, the inscription here can be seen, explaining its place in history:

*An Old Indian Stone Removed From and
Now Overlooking "Powhatan Seat," A Royal
Residence of King Powhatan When Captain
John Smith and His Fellow "Adventurers"
Made the First Permanent English Settlement
In This Country at Jamestown, Virginia 1607.*

*"Powhatans Seat" Was the Residence from
1726–1865 of the Ancestors of Peter H. Mayo
By Whose Daughter This Stone Was
Presented to the Association for the
Preservation of Virginia Antiquities.*

The stone's location overlooks the Fulton Gas Works and railroad yard. It was moved to its present location when the gasworks were built. Some debate whether the three-hundred-year-old stone is authentic, but most agree that the present site is a better place for the stone.

FESTIVAL PARK

Nina Friedman Abady Tribute

Recreation and the arts play major roles in the city's Festival Park, between the Richmond Coliseum and the Sixth Street Marketplace. It also honors one responsible for building camaraderie through this medium. The Nina F. Abady Festival Park features a replica of a plaque bearing her likeness and a partial list of her accomplishments in community, historic and civic endeavors.

Nina Friedman Abady
A Renaissance Woman
1924–1993

There was a world in her dreams
That should have been and yet may be

She believed in Richmond, its people and its future, a city of joy
And harmony, a place to come together and build alliances and
Nurture promise, to learn from one another to celebrate and grow.
Nina's lifting spirit has blessed the city she loved so wisely and
so well and we are all immeasurably the richer.

In remembrance from a grateful community

May 16, 1995.

Ms. Abady was passionate about the arts and her community. She worked enthusiastically as founder and supporter of a number of community projects that helped revitalize downtown. She was a master at getting people together to share their talents and enjoy one other.

Ms. Abady founded Downtown Presents, Friday Cheers, The Big Gig and the Second Street Festival. She was noted for her outward personality and frankness. She was quoted as saying on one occasion, "I don't want to be a spectator. I want to be a participant." She didn't prize possessions, and when asked how she reacted to pressure, she said, "I don't react to it; I cause it." Her days started at 7:30 a.m., she said, "and ended when the meetings end or the band stops playing."

In recognition of her accomplishments, an award is given each year in her name to the fundraiser of the year who has demonstrated utmost excellence in the field of development. The award signifies to individuals, organizations and the greater community that the recipient has garnered the respect and admiration of colleagues throughout the commonwealth for professional and ethical service.

Festival Park also has tributes to Richmond police offices and recognition of the Richmond Blues military unit (see the "Military" and "Law Enforcement" chapters for explanation of these statues).

Dave Hotchkiss Memorial

A monument at Hotchkiss Field on Brooklyn Park Boulevard was placed in a humanitarian act by the Richmond Amateur Baseball Commission. The unpretentious statue was erected to commemorate an early unfortunate event at this location, as described by the inscription:

Hotchkiss Field
A Memorial to
Captain
Dave Hotchkiss
North Richmond
Class AA Baseball team
who
was fatally injured
by a pitched ball on
July 24, 1926.
Erected by the
Richmond Amateur Baseball
Commission

The space today is still very popular. Local citizens congregate there to make use of the gymnasium, ball fields, computer lab and multipurpose room. Located outside the community center are two baseball diamonds, three basketball courts, a large playground, two tennis courts and a swimming pool. Recreation classes are offered in the areas of cultural arts, fitness, dance, crafts, cooking, self-improvement, computer classes, drama, sports, games, hobbies, martial arts, music and do-it-yourself instruction.

MONROE PARK

Monroe Park started as Western Square, when it was much larger. Stretching across Broad Street, its boundaries to the north included such suburbs as Harvietown and Scuffletown. In the mid-1800s, the park held fairs accommodating huge crowds with its large buildings and popular racetrack. During the Civil War, troops camped there, and it was used as a hospital.

After the Civil War, it was just a dusty field with no trees. For a decade or so, it was mainly used by young men playing what was becoming the nation's most popular sport: baseball.

Today, the park is a multi-use area that doubles as a memorial for a variety of notables.

Joseph Bryan

A statue of Joseph Bryan by William Couper is a seven-and-a-half-foot bronze figure. It sits on an eight-and-a-half-foot granite base under the trees in the north end of the park. Erected on June 10, 1911, the tribute is dedicated to one of Richmond's most brilliant businessmen and civic leaders. Mr. Bryan also distinguished himself during the Civil War as one of "Mosby's Men."

Mr. Bryan was a partner to James Dooley. Both men were well known for their generous philanthropic efforts. Bryan also has the distinction of having the most streets named in his honor. North-side thoroughfares Gloucester Road, Laburnum Avenue and Wilmington Avenue are named for Eagle Point, Richmond, and Georgia Island estates.

Not leaving Mr. Bryan's importance to chance, the indirect homage continued. Chatham Street was named for his mother's childhood home. Palmyra Avenue recognizes the town where he first practiced law. Lamont Street honors an oft-used name in his wife's family. Confederate Avenue stretches the deft concept to its maximum, taking its name for the breastworks near the Bryans' Westwood estate that reportedly reminded him of his services with Mosby's raiders.

George Washington Marker

A small stone rests next to the walkway at the northeast section of the park. It marks the spot where the Daughters of the Cinncinatus planted an elm tree in honor of George Washington on February 22, 1932. The tree died, but the memory is preserved. (For a discussion of the statue of General Williams Carter Wickham and the World War II memorial that reside in the park, see the "Military" chapter.)

Pine Camp

People of all ages enjoy the facilities at Pine Camp. Recreation programs and classes are offered in the areas of sports, art, fitness, dance, crafts, games, active adult (seniors) programs and computers, as well as an after-school Fun Klub. The center also hosts a summer camp, special events, workshops and cultural events.

Archenima

Araya Asgedom and Kwabena Ampofo-Anti, two Hampton professors, produced *Archenima*. The name was derived from two sources: "arche" refers to the origin, the primordial, the ancestral and the one, while "anima" refers to the animating life force of all living things.

The artwork, placed at Pine Camp, animates the creative play space at that center, run by the city's Division of Recreation and Parks. The carvings group is composed of three seven-hundred-pound six- by six-foot mahogany figures. The artwork's overall theme concerns self-admiring values. Each figuration relief panel represents a unique aspect of the intellectual, emotional, spiritual and physical skills needed to achieve a positive life.

The artists stated in their proposal their belief that "a fundamental ability of public art is to transform our habitable environments and help unite our diverse communities intellectually, sensually, and culturally." They trusted that the realization of *Archenima* would contribute toward the communal understanding and invite participants and visitors to make the camp a place of creativity.

Darlene Marschak, the program specialist at the camp, suggested that the piece stimulates imagination and play. It was made from a cloth mould after the metal supports were in place. It was intended for interactive play, but it has since been determined to be too dangerous.

CHAPTER 4

Military

Monument Avenue is not the only venue for military statues and monuments. This chapter discovers other tributes to military-connected placements that dot the streets and parks of the city. Although some are Civil War–related remembrances, individuals and units of other conflicts are among them. It is refreshing to contemplate the heroes and outfits of other confrontations. By isolating battle-worn memories, we can have a better recognition of the more peaceful tributes in the city.

HOWITZER

The statue at Park and Grove Avenues and Harrison Street, in the triangular park at the west edge of Virginia Commonwealth University, is a good place to start. The impressive statue honoring the Howitzers is another design of Richmonder William Ludwell Sheppard. Sheppard was an officer in this outfit, and that no doubt influenced his design. Howitzers trace their history to the seventeenth century. This unit lasted until the end of the Civil War in 1865.

Dedicated on December 13, 1892, the monument shows an eight-foot-high artilleryman in bronze mounted on a nine-and-a-half-foot-high Classical-style pedestal, also designed by Mr. Sheppard. The soldier stands

erect, holding his hat in his left hand and the ramrod for a cannon in his right.

A shield of the Confederacy in bronze—with thirteen stars in two crossed bands contained in a wreath of olive leaves—appears on the north side of the statue. The inscription recognizes the longevity of the unit:

FROM BETHEL TO APPOMATTOX

The south side of the statue bears an insignia with a wreath of olive leaves in bronze. Beneath the cannon, the date 1859 denotes the start of the Howitzer division. Also, the Latin motto *Cita mors aut victoria laeta* ("Quick death or glorious victory") is visible.

Facing east, the inscription reads:

To commemorate
the deeds and services
of
The Richmond Howitzers
of the period
1861–1865

The memorial to the cannoneers was sponsored by the Howitzer Association. Casper Buberl, noted for his numerous Civil War statues, made the bronze figure and medallions.

First Regiment Statue

The Park and Stuart Triangle displays a statue honoring the First Regiment, established in 1754. The unit included such notables as Patrick Henry and George Washington in its ranks.

This is another of Ferruccio Legnaioli's work. Placed on May 1, 1930, the seven-foot bronze soldier stands on a granite pedestal surrounded by a manicured hedge. Facing east, the soldier is dressed as a frontiersman, from the fur cap to the leather coat and leggings. He holds a flintlock rifle in both hands in front of him. A coonskin hat sits atop his head, and he strikes a military pose. The figure is modeled after General Lewis, who represents colonial times, in Thomas Crawford's equestrian statue of George Washington at the capitol.

The four sides of the statue describe the impressive history and service of the regiment through seven wars. The eastern plaque reads:

Erected to the Imperishable Memory of the Valiant Fallen of the First Regiment of Virginia Infantry Who through Seven American Wars Endured Hardships with Patience Met Conflict with Constant Courage Did Not Vaunt Their Victories and Steadfastly Kept the Faith with God and Their Country.

The southern plaque reads:

Organized A.D. 1754, with Joshua Fry as Col and With George Washington as Lieutenant Col. The First Regiment of Virginia Fought at Great Meadow and Fort Necessity and Won Praise for Its Steadinesss at Braddock's Defeat, Captured Fort Duquesne and Served Until 1762. In 1775 for the Defense of Virginia. The Regiment Was Reorganized Under the

COMMAND OF PATRICK HENRY. EMBARKED SUBSEQUENTLY INTO THE CONTINENTAL ARMY IT KEPT THE FIELD UNTIL INDEPENDENCE HAD BEEN WON. THE FREEDOM THEN GAINED THE REGIMENT DEFENDED IN THE WAR OF 1812 AND IN THE LATER CONFLICT WITH MEXICO IT CARRIED THE COLORS OF VIRGINIA TRIUMPHANTLY THROUGH THE STREETS OF MONTEREY.

The western plaque reads:

WHEN VIRGINIA JOINED THE CONFEDERATE STATES TO DEFEND THE HONOR AND HER SOVEREIGN RIGHT THE FIRST REGIMENT FORTHWITH VOLUNTEERED FOR DUTY. IT MET THE VANGUARD OF THE FEDERALS, JULY 18, 1861. IT SHARED THE DANGERS OF THE "BLOODY SEVEN DAYS" AND THE LATER TRIUMPHS OF THE CAMPAIGN OF 1862. IT FOUGHT IN MARYLAND AND WITH KEMPER'S BRIGADE OF PICKETT'S DIVISION ARMY OF NORTHERN VIRGINIA. IT CHALLENGED THE CEMETERY BRIDGE AT GETTYSBURG. DECIMATED THERE, IT REJOINED ON MAY 23, 1864 TO STAND AT COLD HARBOR AND ON THE RICHMOND LINE IN TWENTY-TWO ENGAGEMENTS. IT GAVE OF ITS BEST UNTIL IT WAS OVERWHELMED AT APPOMATTOX COURTHOUSE IN 1865.

The northern plaque reads:

THE FIRST REGIMENT OF VIRGINIA MET WITH ZEAL THE CALL OF THE COUNTRY IN THE YEAR 1896. ALL OF ITS UNITS RESPONDED TO THE PRESIDENTS ORDER AND MOBILIZED TO THE BOUNDARY IN MEXICO IN 1916. SUMMONED TO SERVICE IN THE STRUGGLE WITH GERMANY THE REGIMENT THEN BECAME THE FIRST BATTALION OF THE 116TH INFANTRY IN THE TWENTY-NINTH DIVISION. IN OCTOBER 1918 IT WAS EMPLOYED IN THE OFFENSIVE ON THE EAST OF THE MEUSE NORTH OF VERDUN. WHEREAS ITS ADVANCE CAUSED LOSS THAT WERE SUSTAINED IN THE SPIRIT DISPLAYED AT BRADDOCK'S DEFEAT AND IN THE REVOLUTION AND ON THE HILL AT GETTYSBURG. REORGANIZED AFTER THE PEACE OF 1919, THE REGIMENT PLEDGED ITS DEAD TO PRESERVE THEIR IDEALS OF DUTY.

RICHMOND INFANTRY BLUES

Since 1977, a fourteen-and-a-half-foot-tall soldier has stood near the Richmond Coliseum honoring the Richmond Infantry Blues. The National Guard unit formed in 1789 and lasted until 1968. The impressive military figure, sculpted by Colonel Wilford D. Biettiger, stands at parade rest, wearing a Blues uniform, including shake hat and feather plum. A 1903 Springfield rifle is at his right side.

Inscriptions on the base (front and rear) of the statue reflect the activity of the unit, naming each of the wars in which it fought:

War of 1812,
War Between the States,
in the Spanish-American War (1898) and in World Wars I and II,
the Korean War (1950–1953) and the Berlin Crisis (1962).

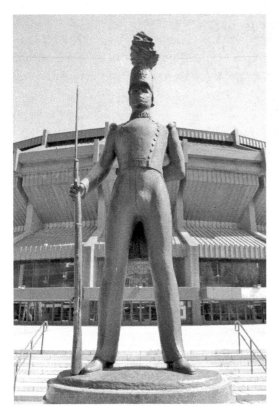

The unit also saw service during Gabriel's Rebellion in 1800, was engaged in another racial incident during the Nat Turner Rebellion of 1831, guarded John Brown after his capture at Harpers Ferry and was mustered into the Confederate army in 1861. In less combative years, the Blues were a popular unit in parades and celebrations in the Richmond area.

The uniforms were originally red, but the association with the former enemy British caused the color to be changed to blue. Accordingly, the unit derived its name from the uniform.

The fashionable unit trained in the 1910 massive brick armory at Sixth and Marshall Streets until 1965. In the 1970s, the lower level was renovated and incorporated into the Sixth Street Market. The second floor was converted to offices. The third floor, where troops trained and drilled, was thrown into the role of storage. Several murals depicting the ceremonies of the Blues are still found painted on two of the walls. Hopefully, someone will develop a way to preserve them. The building was listed on the National Register of Historic Places on May 17, 1976.

GENERAL A.P. HILL

Watching the traffic traverse the roundabout at Laburnum Avenue and Hermitage Road intersection makes it difficult to pay attention to the

imposing statue of a soldier at this site. Confederate general Ambrose Powell Hill (1825–1865), an 1847 graduate of West Point Military Academy, is that soldier.

Hill was an important military figure in the Civil War. He was popular with the rank and file soldiers, who respected his skill, ability and courage. One officer called him "the most lovable of all Lee's generals." Although it was suggested that "his manner was so courteous as almost to lack decision," the only criticism was that his actions were often impetuous—he lacked judgment, not decision. General Robert E. Lee once said that next to Longstreet and Jackson, he considered Hill the best commander he had, adding, "He fights his troops well and takes good care of them."

Born in Culpeper, Virginia, Hill was also an officer in the Mexican-American War and Seminole Wars. He became a general in the Confederate army in 1862. Hill was killed by a Federal soldier in Petersburg, Virginia, on April 2, 1865.

Although there is not full agreement, a Pickett Society investigation and others indicate that Hill was not buried first at Bellegrade Plantation, near Huguenot and Robious Roads in Chesterfield, but rather in an area south of the James River near Bosher Dam. Whichever the case, his remains were unearthed in 1867 and transferred to Hollywood Cemetery. In 1891, the remains were moved again and buried below the statue in an upright stance.

The statue of Hill stands nine and a half feet above a pedestal twenty-four feet high on property donated by Major Lewis Ginter, legendary Richmond financier and philanthropist. Pegram's Battalion was instrumental in having the statue erected, and Casper Burberl of New York finished the bronze. It is said to be the only statue in Richmond for which the subject is buried beneath the honor. The front of the monument carries this inscription:

Born in Culpepper Co.
November 9th 1825
Killed before Petersburg
April 2nd 1865.

The back of the monument reads:

His remains
were interred here
June 24, 1891.

FITZHUGH LEE

The statue of Fitzhugh Lee, Confederate general during the American Civil War and commander of the cavalry of the Army of Northern Virginia during the last months of the conflict, was originally planned to be more elaborate in Monroe Park. The son of "Lighthouse Harry" Lee and nephew

of General Robert E. Lee, his honor was to be life-size and stand on a granite seventy-foot-diameter pedestal.

If dollars were forthcoming, secondary figures around the base would have been added to symbolize Lee's various military roles, similar to the statue of George Washington outside the capitol by Thomas Crawford. Lee served as governor of Virginia from 1886 to 1890. He never gained fame as an innovative military tactician or strategist, but he achieved modest success during his Confederate service. He later became a national hero thanks to his well-publicized promotion of American interests as United States consul general in Havana, Cuba, on the eve of the Spanish-American War (1898).

Despite his accomplishments, he didn't fare as well as his better-known relative, Robert E. Lee. Completed by Richmonder Edward V. Valentine, the six-foot-diameter Greek cross became a compromise as a result of limited funds. It was erected by the 7th Corps Veterans Association Auxiliary in 1905 and commands a prestigious position in the park so as to be seen from the street.

GENERAL WILLIAMS CARTER WICKHAM

The statue of Williams Carter Wickham (1820–1888) was given to the city by the general's comrades in the Confederate army and employees of the Chesapeake and Ohio Railway in 1891. Illustrating his versatility, following his name on the statue, the inscription reads, "Soldier, Statesman, Patriot, Friend." Monroe Park was chosen to display the statue, where it remains today.

Wickham, a lawyer, judge and politician, was also a brigadier general. He served as president of the Chesapeake Railroad and was a member of the Republican Party. He also took a congressional seat in the Hampton Roads Peace Conference. The conference failed because President Lincoln refused to condone any plan that permitted the continuance of slavery.

The spot where Wickham stands has an interesting background, as Richmond's Washington Monument once stood at this position.

In 1870, one of the six copies made of Jean-Antoine Houdon's *George Washington* by James Hubard was given to the city by Hubard's widow and became known as the "Washington Monument." In 1883, the city council received notice from Mrs. Hubard alerting them that she had sold the bronze to Samuel Spahr Laws, then president of the University of Missouri in Columbia, Missouri. It stayed there until 1889, when Laws retired and returned to his native Ohio. Laws took the statue with him and donated it to the Cincinnati Art Museum.

It had a brief stint in the Corcoran Art Gallery in Washington, from which Laws attempted to sell the statue to the United States government when he was ninety-six years old. The government failed to meet his price for the sale, and he donated the statue to his alma mater, Miami University in Oxford, Ohio. It remains on display at that institution to this day.

VIGIL

At a side entrance to the McGuire Veterans Hospital Medical Building (12011 Broad Rock Road) stands a statue with an interesting background. Placed in 1983, the layout for the presentation comes from a real-life story about the sculptor Lester Van Winkle.

Vigil, a cast silicon bronze grouping of three images, was born from a photograph of the artist's mother while his father was in the service. The scene contains a pot or crucible in the center branching into the American flag (ten feet at its highest point), symbolizing national growth. A female figure stands awaiting the veteran's return to active life. She represents gentleness, patience and compassion. A dog on the right side of the woman stands guard, depicting vigilance, determination and tenacity.

Van Winkle's model, a similar rendition, appears in miniature in a small museum at the main entrance of this institution. This version is not identical to the statue. That came about because Van Winkle, who was at the time instructor at VCU's top-ranked School of Sculpture, ran into an unusual problem before being able to complete the statue.

The placement committee objected to a chair used in the grouping. It wanted to avoid any controversy, particularly in light of the spinal work being done at the hospital. Somewhat confused by the notion, Mr. Van Winkle complied with the changes, and it has remained a popular attraction ever since.

See more of Van Winkle's talent in the "Law Enforcement" and "Virginia Commonwealth University" chapters.

WORLD WAR II MEMORIAL

On the northwest corner of Monroe Park, the World War II Memorial lists the names of almost six hundred Richmond men and women who made the supreme sacrifice during that conflict. The services are separated—U.S. Army, U.S. Marine Corps and U.S. Navy, with the appropriate names listed under each. Framed in a wall of brick, the statue was erected by Post No. 1 of the American Legion.

MEMORY (VIRGINIA WAR MEMORIAL)

The Virginia War Memorial on Jefferson Davis Highway on Bellevue Avenue at Rowe Street remembers Virginia veterans who gave the supreme sacrifice. A twenty-two-foot statue representing motherhood stands on a base of more than two hundred soil samples from American military cemeteries.

Carved from 100,000 pounds of white marble, *Memory*, the female figure, reflects both the sorrow and pride felt by Virginians for their fallen brothers and sisters.

Designed by Leo Friedlander and sculpted by Joseph Campo and William Knapp, the memorial was originally erected in 1955 but has since been enlarged to now honor 11,638 Virginia heroes, whose names are engraved on the glass and stone walls. The present drawing board includes plans to include those who met the same fate in the "War on Terror," which will unfortunately add more than one hundred who lost their lives in Iraq and Afghanistan.

At the base of *Memory* is the "Torch of Liberty," the eternal flame that represents patriotism. Headed by General Alexander Vandergrife, the United States Army and the widows and mothers of deceased Congressional Medal of Honor recipients from Virginia lit this torch in February 1956.

Just outside the south end of the shrine, seven flags fly: U.S. Army, U.S. Marine Corps, U.S. Navy, U.S. Coast Guard, U.S. Air Force, Merchant Marine and the flag of the Virginia War Memorial. In the center of this semicircle of flags flies the POW/MIA flag in memory of those prisoners of war and soldiers missing in action not yet recovered. To the north fly the national and state flags.

Special celebrations are held at the memorial on important military anniversaries. Programs are held for Memorial Day, Armed Forces Day, Veterans Day, Pearl Harbor Day and so on. A museum and library are available to visitors.

The recent addition of the eighteen-thousand-square-foot Paul and Phyllis Galanti Education Center adds a new dimension to the memorial. The center provides a variety of internal and outreach programs, artifacts, research materials, *Virginians at War* documentaries, exhibitions, films, seminars and ceremonies. The center brings numerous patriotic educational programs to a wide range of citizens. This is truly a monument on the move.

It is ever so appropriate that this extensive center has been named for two American heroes. Paul and Phyllis Galanti each served the United States beyond the call of duty during and since the Vietnam War. It is a modest way to ensure that their sacrifice and service protecting our and others' freedoms will never be forgotten.

CONFEDERATE SOLDIERS AND SAILORS MONUMENT

Libby Hill Park at Twenty-ninth and Main Streets, with access from Broad Street, is one of three original parks in the city. Formerly called Marshall Square, the park provides a view south that is said to resemble that of overlooking the Thames in Richmond, England.

The Confederate Soldiers and Sailors Monument has risen above these grounds since its unveiling on May 30, 1894. It was a gift of the Soldiers and Sailors Association to the gallant men who defended our cause, with Fitz Lee as chief marshal. More than 100,000 were reported to have witnessed the occasion.

The statue was placed after encountering several obstacles. Fundraising dried up after the initial thrust and had to be bailed out by selling as souvenirs miniature muskets, sabers and other assorted military-related paraphernalia as an inducement to obtain additional contributions. Finally, the state and corporations combined to assist with the final cost of $30,000.

Modeled after Pompey's Pillar, the tower of the Roman general Pompey the Great, it was done by W.L. Sheppard. The granite column rises to ninety feet atop thirteen stone cylinders representing the thirteen Confederate states. A seventeen-foot-tall soldier stands on the top.

Sheppard was a late second choice; internationally renowned sculptor Moses Ezekiel was the frontrunner to do the statue. Months of haggling over the design and compensation finally wearied the committee members to the point that they replaced the better-known sculptor.

Lighting was added to the statue on November 4, 1964, with Mayor Crowe presiding over the festivities.

CARILLON

At the end of Blanton Avenue, on the perimeter of Byrd Park, stands a structure that is 240 feet high, with fifty-six bells playing fifty-six notes. The idea for the carillon was conceived by a group of World War I veterans. Designed by noted Boston architect Ralph Adams Cram, it is his interpretation of the Italian campanile in Georgian classicism.

An act by the Virginia General Assembly creating a war memorial commission during the 1924 session paved the way for the memorial. The legislative body stated that the committee was formed for the purpose of erecting in the city of Richmond a memorial to the men and women who served in the war.

After considerable discussion, the present structure was decided on. As fundraising began, the assembly, wary of too great a financial responsibility in the matter, stipulated that no appropriations would be made by the state until two conditions were met. First, private funds would be needed to purchase bells for the carillon, amounting to a sum of nearly $75,000. Second, provisions for the perpetual care of the memorial needed to be made by the City of Richmond or a private group or association.

Both requirements were met, and construction began on land in Byrd Park donated by the City of Richmond. The balance of the $325,000 cost to build the carillon was a joint venture of the City of Richmond and the Commonwealth of Virginia. World Life Insurance Society also contributed significantly. Built by the John Taylor Bell Foundry in England, the memorial was dedicated in 1932 to commemorate those who served in World War I.

Originally, sixty-six bells played fifty-three notes; three of the top thirteen notes had duplicate bells in an unsuccessful effort to make the sound louder. When the carillon was renovated in the 1970s, the thirty-three bells that played the highest twenty-one notes were recast into twenty-one new bells

with thicker profiles than the originals. This produced a better sound, and now there are fifty-three bells for fifty-three notes.

A shallow pool was planned to be built to reflect the carillon, hence the dug-out area in front of the carillon, but money ran out before it could be completed.

Since 1981, the carillon has been mostly closed, catering to an occasional charity ball and the annual nativity pageant.

WORLD WAR I MEMORIAL

A plaque on a flagpole, less than one mile north of the carillon, honors the Richmond soldiers who paid the ultimate sacrifice in World War I. The inscription reads:

Those who gave their lives for
God and Country
1917–1918
In honor of the men and
women who gave their lives in
World War I for the principles
of justice, freedom and
democracy.
Erected by their comrades of
the fine Richmond posts of the
American Legion
1926.

The other sides of the plaque list in alphabetical order those who perished. In a sign of the times, following the last name and listed in a separate section, another alphabetical list begins under the heading "Colored." Let it be a reminder of how far we have come to now have only American soldiers.

CHAPTER 5

Law Enforcement

T he art of law enforcement is not restricted to the function of keeping order and protecting citizens. Throughout the Richmond area, this point is reinforced many times over by the various statues, murals, and paintings that appear in precincts, in parks, and other significant locations. Several examples are cited.

THIN BLUE LINE

Thin Blue Line, on the east wall of the Richmond Police Department headquarters (200 West Grace Street) in the Monroe District, has had its detractors, but it has ultimately prevailed. The twelve-foot tall, 1,300-pound stainless steel sculpture of a police officer's head is by artist Michael Stutz. The officer has looked down on those who pass since being dedicated on February 10, 2005.

Stutz said that he set out to create an authoritative flavor befitting a strong police force seeking to take charge of the city's crime, and at the same time, he wanted "an expressive human quality reflecting the heroic everyman spirit of police officers." Stutz used about five thousand welds for the figure. The cost of the piece was nearly $140,000.

Thin Blue Line is often used as a symbol of support for police officers; however, in this case, the placement was clouded in controversy. Stutz

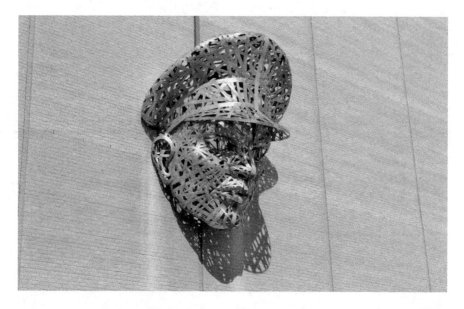

explained in the case of the Grace Street rendition, the blue line was intended to depict the separation of order and chaos. Although it wasn't universally received that way, it remains at its initial location as the anxiety over the piece has gradually subsided.

THOMAS F. (MONGO) MCMAHON MEMORIAL

It is not always the effort of the city or the arts commission that gets memorials placed. A good exception is found in Church Hill at Libby Hill Park. The "Mongo's Stone" there represents the effort of citizens and police officers working together in their fight against crime.

The four-thousand-pound stone, taken from Richmond's turning basin (see the "James River" section) carries the inscription:

In memory
of
Officer THOMAS F
"Mongo"
McMAHON
killed in the line of duty
on
October 14, 1998
Dedicated
by his
family and friends.

Such an honor has to be earned. McMahon was considered a member of the community, quick with a joke and even quicker with a helping hand. His love of life is evidenced by his camaraderie with the citizens on his beat. He was known for his harmonica playing and his sharing of 250,000 Christmas lights on his Henrico County home; he was also a happy barbecuer on weekends. From this came the affectionate nickname "Mongo."

McMahon never asked for a transfer out of the Church Hill neighborhood. One member of the neighborhood summed up McMahon's twenty years of service: "His devotion to our crime watch and this neighborhood will never be forgotten. To all who did not know him, we ask respect and possibly your best joke."

SUNDAY

We don't normally think of a sculpture being in a detention center, but it happened in Richmond, and it turned out to be quite meaningful for the occupants at the Seventeenth Street Oliver Hill Detention Center. The experiment was the creation of local artist Lester Van Winkle.

His rendition at this location, *Sunday*, is a dog with a ball in its mouth. The dog gazes about the small courtyard from his chosen chair among five, perhaps searching for a companion with whom to play. The surface of the animal's head has been rubbed smooth and shiny by the youngsters. A large bronze ball rests on the dirt center of the square. The eye is led to the remaining structures.

The four basic forms surrounding the animal represent laws, right and wrong. They are designed for further compatibility. A cube, cone and sphere rest on a concrete table lined with a stainless steel border. The pieces throw off warmth of access and availability to the institutional setting. The pet adds credibility to the theme, figuratively removing the confinement. Benches and chairs send out an invitation to join the scene, to become a part—perhaps something that society had neglected.

One wonders how many arms have been placed around the neck of this dog and how many hours have been spent in contemplation on the enticing bench. How many times have the simple forms been rearranged in an effort to untangle a problem or motivated the design of a new creation, reaching out to connect the thought of hope for another chance?

Evidence of the effectiveness is apparent with the additions that enhance the courtyard. Attractive tables with attached seating and a large grill get extensive use, accenting the thesis. The courtyard has become a place of rehabilitation where a troubled youth can gain acceptance and have a chance to grow as contributing citizens. The chief administrator endorsed the result enthusiastically.

The scene sends off an air of positive assurance. When asked about the creation, the artist's modesty rang out with these words: "It's the stuff I like to do." The presentation of the still-life landscape, interlocking geometry and organic forms has a lot more to say. Something has been accomplished.

Oliver Hill Courthouse

Next door, continuing the recognition of Mr. Oliver Hill, the courthouse bearing his name contains another positive message conspicuously hung on the entrance wall. *In Pursuit of Growth and Achievement* has three seven-hundred-pound six- by six-foot mahogany carvings, created by nationally recognized African American artist Ayokunle Odelege.

Trained at the School of Sculpture of Virginia Commonwealth University, Mr. Odelege presents a theme of self-admiring values. Each of the three figuration wood relief panels represents unique aspects of the intellectual, emotional, spiritual and physical skills needed to achieve a positive life:

- Development of creative and competitive skills.
- Address striving for education, development of professional skill and respect for laws of our country.
- Stress importance of family life, spiritual guidance and honest work.

With the May 1, 1997 unveiling of this work, the Oliver Hill Courthouse has enjoyed a dynamic and inspiring artwork that reflects on the positive work accomplished in this important institution.

POLICE MEMORIAL

Behind the Sixth Street Market at the Coliseum stands a 1,200-pound, eight-foot bronze figure of a Richmond policeman. This statue by Maria Juliana Kirby-Smith was dedicated during National Police Week in May 1987 to honor the twenty-six officers who had died in the line of duty. It carries the inscription:

> *We the people of Richmond present this memorial in recognition of police officers who afford us their protection. Those officers named here are remembered particularly for making the supreme sacrifice by giving their lives in the line of duty.*

[twenty-eight names listed]

> *...We here highly resolve that these dead shall not have died in vain.*

The statue depicts a police officer rescuing a child. He is shown walking down steps with the child in his arms (the child, minus a shoe, is holding

a stuffed teddy bear in her right hand). Sergeant J. Harvey Burke, killed in 1925, is that officer. Burke was shot while trying to quiet a domestic quarrel just one block from the memorial site. Personal stories connected to the statue offer further heartwarming appreciation of the placement.

The Miller & Rhoads Department Store provided space on the third-floor for the sculpture. Milton Burke, a treasured employee and notable leading citizen for many years, was responsible for the Miller & Rhoads donation. His father, Sergeant Burke, was the sixth officer to die in the line of duty. The younger Burke raised more than $6,000 toward the statue by sending out a homemade flyer to friends and relatives asking them to donate dollars in his father's name.

The statue was presented to the city by Edwin Stephenson, son of patrolman Edwin H. Stephenson Jr., who was also killed answering a call.

No coverage of this statue would be complete without the story of the sculptor's joke: she added a note to the back of the officer's shoe. Not funny to the authorities, they ordered the message "PIG-oint resistant" removed.

The state police department, Richmond Academy and the Counties of Henrico and Chesterfield have also erected memorials to their law officers who lost their lives in service.

CHAPTER 6

Scattered About the City

Many of the entries that assist in telling the history of Richmond are found hidden within various corners of the city. We can't let them escape. Our discovery ends with a look at these important contributors located at the outskirts of the city.

ARNOLD'S PICKET

Upon Mulberry Street and Grove Avenue, a two-foot-high marker commemorates the spot where Colonel Nicholas supposedly drove Benedict Arnold's troops away in 1781. The monument is the second-oldest outdoor non-cemetery monument in the city. Some say John Nicholas Jr. executed the marker himself in an act of fictional self-glory; the marker is also thought to have been moved from an original location.

Erected by the Sons of the Revolution in 1834, the marker experienced deterioration and at one point vanished. The pylon turned up later at the Empire Monumental Works, a division of Empire Granite. It was erected again in 1948 and then again in 1991. Today, the original inscription is carried by the granite replacement. Only the north face of the statue facing away from the street lacks an inscription. On the south face, it reads:

Arnold's
Picket
driven in
Jany 4th 1781
By
Col. J. Nicholas

On the west face, it reads:

> *This pylon, re-created in granite and containing*
> *a replica of the original 1834 inscription, was*
> *re-dedicated April 17, 1991,*
> *by the Sons of the Revolution in the State of Virginia.*

On the east face, it reads:

> *The central pylon was erected about 1834 to mark*
> *the site in this vicinity where Benedict Arnold's attack*
> *during the Revolution was repulsed.*
> *The scene was re-erected by the Sons of the Revolution in the State of*
> *Virginia in 1948.*

BUD AND SEED GROUP

The steel sculptures at the beginning of the Virginia Capital Trail are the creation of David Boyajian of Connecticut. Three nine-and-a-half- to eleven-foot-tall plantlike structures called the *Bud and Seed Group*, each with a singular "blossom" on a flexing "stem," are located in a hidden space behind the floodwall, opposite from Bottom's Up Pizza at 1710 Dock Street.

Unfortunately, it appears that they were fabricated in steel too thin to withstand handling by people. Shortly after installation, all of the structures were damaged. One piece was found crimped and bent slightly forward. The other two showed breaks in the welds.

When Boyajian attempted to repair the art, he apparently added metal reinforcement "splints" and welded them on without smoothing the spot welds or closing gaps in the angled iron repairs. The art commission has determined that the repairs were not sufficient and potentially ruined the artwork. "The repair looked almost like two different people did the work," said William Hutchins, a member of the commission. The three pieces, which came to Richmond after spending a year in a more protected garden setting at Longwood University, cost about $20,000. So far, the sculptures have cost about $1,700 in repairs.

The Virginia Capital Trail is a fifty-five-mile recreational path being built between Richmond and Williamsburg, and the $2.3 million section that starts where the statues are located extends about 3,500 feet from the floodwall along Dock Street near Eighteenth Street to Great Shiplock Park.

Directly across from the *Bud and Seed Group* sits an attractive stone memorial to one who was a strong proponent of the trail and a major contributor to Virginia public health, as evidenced by an extensive inscription.

CARL WILLIAM ARMSTRONG MEMORIAL

This memorial holds the ashes of Mr. Armstrong and bears the following inscription:

> *In Memory of*
> *Carl William Armstrong*
> *February 25, 1950–March 5, 2009*
>
> *Our son, father, husband*
> *Brother, friend, colleague*
>
> *Revered Virginia Public Health Physician*
> [four steps, walking forward, are presented]
> *Strong proponent of the*
> *Virginia Capital Trail Project*
>
> *Long standing member of the*
> *Richmond Area Bicycling Association*
> *Tandem Captain of "Blazing Saddles"*
>
> [an embossed bicycling pair is presented]
>
> *Carl, your impact has enriched many*
> *Lives and will be felt for generations*
> *We dedicate this respite in your honor*

Dr. Armstrong was eulogized by the Virginia legislature for his four decades of significant contributions to the field of health as a talented epidemiologist and a founding member of Virginians Improving Patient Care and Safety, which works to prevent medical errors, measure ways to improve the clinical quality of patient care and enhance emergency preparedness by linking hospitals and public health leaders. His insightful writing about end-of-life care was also acknowledged.

CONNECTICUT

Connecticut looks over the James River from its perch above 2700 East Cary Street, where it has resided since November 6, 2010. The fiberglass and resin composition measuring twenty-five by thirteen feet weighs in at 2,400 pounds and is the creation of local sculptor Paul DiPasquale.

The giant Indian brave, whose initial unveiling was intended for a spot along the Potomac River in Washington, D.C., had an interesting beginning before it made its Richmond debut peering out over the Boulevard from a choice spot as an appropriate mascot for the Richmond Braves baseball team.

Connecticut became a reality when the ever-creative DiPasquale sold fifty "etching dividends." The sculptor received $200 for each for a promise that he would pay them back when the sculpture was sold, and as further arrangement, they could keep the prints as dividends. This started what has turned out to be a traveling existence for the statue.

The original site for placement didn't work out; however, the publicity of the dividend plan gained the attention of retail chain Best Products, which contracted for the brave to be placed on the roof of its Washington, D.C., store. It was unveiled to a national television and media audience in September 1983.

The expiration of the lease to Best Products coincided with the opening of the Diamond in Richmond, and DiPasquale lent the sculpture to the Richmond Metropolitan Authority in June 1985. After two years of free display, Signet Bank purchased the piece from the sculptor and then donated it back to RMA, where it remained popular until another move was necessitated when the Diamond was taken over by Squirrels (the name for the new baseball team).

The present placement on the Lucky Strike building was one of three finalist spots for the then twenty-five-year-old brave. Two high schools, Powhatan (Indians) and Henrico (Warriors), were the other entrants. It was decided that the position overlooking the river would provide more visibility to the public. It also helped that a news release from O'dell Associates noted that *Connecticut* was a native Indian word, derived from *Quinnehtukqut*, which translates to "beside the long tidal river."

The brave was recognized by the American Institute of Architects and Greater Richmond Area Commercial Real Estate as an award-winning historical adaptive reuse project for its new location.

THE DANCING MAN

A dancing man statue, donated in 1978 by the principal of Bellevue School (2301 East Grace Street), adds a lively entrance to the building. Within view of the popular St. John's Church, where Patrick Henry uttered his famous words, he is often mistaken for the more admired dancer Bill "Bojangles" Robinson. This location includes a museum that, some say, upstages the sculpture.

The depository inside the school chronicles the story of two women who played important roles in the history of the Virginia capital in contrasting ways. Elizabeth Van Lew was a notorious spy for the Federal troops during the Civil War, when Richmond was the capital of the Confederacy. Early on, she assisted Union soldiers in escaping through a tunnel from the Van Lew mansion, which was originally at this address.

To avoid Confederate interference, Van Lew kept a low profile. She let her hair grow wild and mumbled to herself on the streets. Confederate officials regarded her as eccentric rather than dangerous. That would change as her role increased.

Not proud of the covert activity that took place at this address, the city demolished the mansion where Van Lew and her family had resided. The act was said to have been one of malice due to the disdain for Van Lew and her activity against the Confederate cause. The property first became a sanatorium, but it was soon demolished without opposition and replaced by the school.

The second woman covered in the museum is Maggie Lena Walker. Despite being born into humble circumstances, she overcame her modest start and the many adversities she experienced to build a highly respectable reputation for entrepreneurial skills and compassion. Through her business acumen, she attained national prominence by establishing a newspaper and becoming the first black female president of a bank. The bank she started still exists today. Her dedication to the community won further acclaim, particularly in race relations and finance.

How did it come about that women with such diverse backgrounds would be honored at the same place? The museum clears up the mystery, explaining that during the period the Van Lew family occupied the mansion, Walker's mother was a trusted servant. On July 15, 1867, she gave birth to a bubbling baby girl who was to become one of the city's most respected and famous ladies.

CRADLE

A pair of hands holding the city sits at the headquarters of the Richmond Ambulatory Authority on Hermitage Road where Overbook Road ends. *Cradle*, done by Allan Rosenbaum, at the time an instructor at Virginia Commonwealth University's School of Art, was intended for inside use in a smaller form. When the model was reviewed, Mr. Rosenbaum was asked to prepare a larger statue in bronze for outside placement. His response was, "One of the great joys at this point for me after working with ceramics for 30 years is to be confronted with these challenges. The last thing that I want to do is only the things that I know."

The stunning piece symbolizes the role that the Richmond Ambulance Authority plays for the city. It is Mr. Rosenbaum's first work in bronze. It was well received, but this somewhat obscure location has denied its full potential for significant recognition.

GILBERT ROBERTSON

On the northeast corner of North Boulevard and Kensington Avenue, a stone marker erected on October 6, 1987, honors a man known to many longtime Richmond residents. Gilbert Robertson (1909–1988), a multiple amputee black man, stood on this corner for more than fifty years, selling flowers to citizens who were visiting family and friends at Retreat and Johnston Willis Hospitals, both located near his stand at the time.

Despite his disability, Mr. Robertson always greeted his customers and those who passed by with a smile and a friendly greeting. After his death in 1985, citizens of the neighborhood placed the marker in his honor at this spot. In full recognition of his pleasant personality and work ethic, it has been kept manicured to this day as a tribute to his influence and contribution to the area.

BRIDGE ABUTMENT

Less than one block away, on the 2800 block of Kensington Avenue, another marker stands innocently outside the Historic Resources Building. The bridge abutment is another one of those Civil War mementos that sometimes escape detection.

At one time, the standing pillar was part of a bridge that took travelers over the Anna River on Telegraph Road, at the time part of the main road from Richmond to Washington, near Ashland. It has further historical significance as the place where Robert E. Lee and his forces held off Ulysses Grant and his troops from crossing during the Wilderness Campaign, thus delaying their capture of Richmond.

The plaque on the column reads:

North Anna
River Bridge
Built
1926
Virginia State Highway Commission.
H.G. Shirley, Chairman

Wade H. Massie,   *I. Walke Truxun*
A.J. Huff,   *R.B. Sproul*

C.S. Mullen, Chief Engineer
W.R. Glidden, Bridge Engineer

[seal of Virginia]

SHRINER HOLDING CHILD

At the Acca Shrine Temple (1712 Bellevue Avenue), a proud shriner holds a child in front of the building. Placed in 2005, it represents all that shriners stand for. It carries the inscription:

Acca Temple gratefully acknowledges those groups and Individuals who
through their generous
Donations made possible the addition of the "Editorial without Words"
statue to our foundation

[the donors' names are listed]

[the officers of local shrines are listed]

A note at the bottom reads:

A special thanks to the Lady's Fund Raising Projects
Larry R. Koon—Potentate

An international organization with a membership approaching 400,000, the shriners are best known for sponsoring eighteen orthopedic hospitals and three burn hospitals—one that provides orthopedic burn and spinal injury care where children under eighteen can receive quality treatment free of charge. Shriners sponsor the only spinal cord injury units in the nation designed specifically for children and adolescents.

These units are funded by gifts, income from the endowment fund, hospital funds, fundraising events and the annual assessment paid by every shriner. To date, more than 750,000 children have been served, and more than $7 billion has been directed to the program.

KUGEL

The *Kugel* at the Science Museum (2500 Broad Street) has fascinated visitors since its first installment in 2003. The sculpture from Kusser Granite Works, Germany, is a large granite ball representing Earth and the moon at a scale of about one foot to one thousand miles. Nine feet in diameter and weighing in at about twenty-nine tons, it is recognized by *Guinness World Records* as the world's largest floating-ball sculpture. Supported by a very thin film of water, no belts, pulleys or rubber wheels are involved in the rotation, thus requiring all of its measurements and movements to remain precise and perfectly balanced.

The water flow is set to push the perfectly balanced spherical rock from a spherical concave base with exactly the same curvature at 33.81 pounds per square inch, less than your faucet at home. Regardless of the weight of the *Kugel*, it is lubricated by the film of water and the ball spins. Even a

child could change the course of a floating ball of several tons, but when left alone, it would return to its normal rotation.

Sounds easy, but sometimes the precision breaks down. Carved from an eighty-six-ton block of South African black granite by the same company, the first ball was just a bit smaller at about eight feet, nine inches in diameter, and it was floated by a jet stream on a base of granite. This original ball began to crack and was shut down the next year. Fortunately, the loss was covered by insurance, and the ball was replaced without cost to the museum. A second dedication took place for the present replacement in October 2005.

Kusser didn't want the original ball back, so it stayed at the museum. Private funds paid to move it to a new location, where it was placed with the crack horizontal so that it wouldn't break apart. It can be seen for free, or if you have a big garden, you might be able to negotiate this addition for your daily enjoyment.

ABRAHAM LINCOLN AND SON

Abraham Lincoln hasn't received the same recognition in Richmond statuary demonstrated in other (mostly northern) cities. However, he is depicted in a

life-size bronze statue at Richmond National Battlefield Park (at Tredegar). The piece shows Lincoln and his twelve-year-old son, Tad, sitting on a bench during their historic visit to Richmond on April 4–5, 1865. The two toured the burned-out Confederate capitol, the White House of the Confederacy and Capitol Square, but little of his visit was recorded. He apparently never visited the burned-out Tredegar Iron Works.

The rock for the 2,800-square-foot, five-foot-high elliptical backdrop wall was given by the City of Richmond from leftover material from the construction of the turning basin. The wall carries the inscription, "To Bind Up the Nation's Wounds," a passage from President Lincoln's second inaugural address.

Created by sculptor David French, the statue was a gift from the United States Historical Society. Funds were raised through donations and the selling of 750 miniature versions of the statue at $875 each. The intent, in the society's words, was "to symbolize the African American perspectives of the Civil War." The dedication took place in April 2003, but not without opposition.

Opponents of the statue felt that the commemoration of Lincoln's visit into Richmond was arrogance representing the glory of a proud victor. Robert H. Kline, chairman of the historical society, summed up what became the prevailing view in his dedication remarks, stating, "The purpose of the statue was to symbolize reconciliation for a war that still echoes and creates division. He came on a mission of peace and reconciliation and I think the statue will serve that purpose for a very long time."

John Boone Trotti

Though gargoyles ordinarily wouldn't qualify as legitimate monument discovery, an exception is granted when they are designed around an important individual. At the Union Theological Seminary, on land donated by Lewis Ginter, a likeness of retired librarian John Boone Trotti oversees the seminary library.

Trotti served as librarian at this institution from 1968 to 2002 after earning a bachelor's degree at Davidson College, a Bachelor of Divinity degree at Union Theological Seminary in Richmond, a master's degree in library science from the University of North Carolina and his doctorate in the Old Testament from Yale University.

Dr. Trotti taught at Yale and Randolph-Macon Woman's College and served as pastor of Altavista Presbyterian Church before returning to

his alma mater to expand the Spence Library and oversee the design and construction of the William Smith Morton Library, which opened in 1997.

He was the recipient of the 2012 Award of Excellence in Theological Education and was honored by the General Assembly of Presbyterian Church (USA) as one who has made an outstanding lifetime contribution to theological education in and for the Presbyterian Church (USA).

Throughout his twenty-nine years, Trotti led a program that contributed more than 135,000 volumes to libraries in 103 institutions in fifty-nine countries and sparked the creation of the American Theological Book Redistribution Project wherein many libraries share print resources with their international counterparts. Trotti was still involved in leadership of the programs in his retirement. Unfortunately, he died as this text was being prepared (on February 2, 2013), at age ninety-one.

MOVIELAND

Movieland is one of Richmond's newest entertainment centers, taking over a large complex on North Boulevard just south of the Diamond. It has made

an effort to become a part of the monumental history of Richmond with a set of beams from the early building where it entertains Richmonders today. Outside the entrance, old metal beams are accented by a plaque telling us the significance of the display:

MOVIELAND
A Bow Tie Cinema

This building was once the home of the Richmond
Locomotive Works, one of the world's most
Famous steam locomotive builders.

Steam engines powered the industrial revolution
In the United States and Richmond made steam
Locomotives carried an enormous quantity of
Manufactured products across the continent and
Around the world.

The pieces you see here were all integral parts of
The Richmond Locomotive Works assembly line
Which manufactured great American steam engines
In this building from 1887 to 1927.

Symbolism

A rtists have a way of challenging our thought process. They have a language of their own. It is often a shortcut method of getting a point across, much like the texting approach of today. Getting the point across in this manner was perhaps developed from the necessity of reducing size and amount of verbiage. Some say that it resulted from the need to communicate with an audience with limited education and no reading skills. Symbols were fashioned to better transfer ideas so that the message of the sender was the one received.

The decoration of a monument or a marker may be a sacred or secular symbol; a civic, social, professional or a military emblem; a pictorial delineation; or some graphic record of an event or career. It could be a coat of arms, a college seal or fraternity emblem. It may be a state or national flower associated with the honored person or event. There is no limit to the source of ideas and suggestions for personalizing a memorial with symbolical decoration.

The list of symbols explained here might be used to succinctly clarify the message and assist you the next time you view a statue in detail.

- anchor: hope, seaman
- angels: rebirth, resurrection, protection, judgment, wisdom, mercy, divine love
- ankh: eternal life, peace, truth
- arch: victory in death, being rejoined with partner in heaven

- arrow: mortality, the dart of death
- axe: the weapon of death
- azalea: temperance
- bay leaves: victory over death
- beehive: domestic virtues, education, faith, abundance in the promised land, piety
- bell: mourning
- bird: eternal life, winged soul, spirituality, rebirth
- book: the divine word or one's accomplishments
- broken or draped column: early death, grief
- burning flame: life or resurrection
- butterfly: resurrection
- candlestick: devotion, Christ as the light of the world
- caterpillar: life, metamorphosis
- Celtic cross: faith, eternity
- chain with three links: trinity, faith, odd fellows
- cherub: a winged child of undeterminable sex
- circle: eternity
- column: noble life
- conch shell: wisdom, reincarnation
- cornucopia: abundance
- cross: faith, resurrection
- crown: glory, life after death
- crown on skull: triumph over death
- cup or chalice: the sacrament
- cypress: hope, Christ child's innocence, childhood
- dolphin: resurrection, salvation, bearer of souls across water to heaven
- door: entrance to heaven
- dove: love, purity, resurrection, the Holy Spirit
- drapery or pall: mourning or mortality
- eagle: courage, faith, generosity, contemplation, military
- eye: humility
- female figure: sorrow, grief
- finger pointing downward: calling the earth to witness
- finger pointing upward: pathway to heaven, heavenly reward
- fish: faith, life, spiritual nourishment
- flag: military, patriotism
- fleur-de-lis: perfection, light, life, royalty

- flower (general): life's frailty, immortality
- flying bird: rebirth
- frog: worldly pleasure, sin
- garland: victory over death
- grapes: sacrifice immortality
- Grim Reaper: inevitability of death
- gun: military service
- hair: flowing penitence
- hands clasped: farewell, hope of meeting in eternity
- harp: hope, instrument of angels
- heart: love, devotion, sorrow, joy, mortality, piety
- heart, flaming: religious fervor
- heart pierced by sword: Virgin Mary, Christ, repentance
- helmet: military service, strength, protection
- horse: strength, courage
- horseshoe: protection against evil
- hourglass: swift passage of time, temperance
- "IHS": eternity, Christian symbol ("in his service")
- iris: rebirth, the Virgin Mary, light, hope
- ivy: fidelity, attachment, undying affection, eternal life
- lamb: innocence (especially on a child's grave), resurrection, Jesus
- laurel leaves: triumph
- lily: purity, sometimes chastity
- lily of the valley: rebirth, Virgin Mary
- lion: courage, bravery, strength
- lotus: purity, resurrection, perfect beauty, spiritual revelation
- Masonic compass and set square: Freemasons, uprightness, judgment
- menorah: divine wisdom
- military emblem: a soldier
- mirror: truth, knowledge
- mistletoe: immortality
- moon: death, rebirth, victory, sorrow of the Crucifixion
- mother and child: charity, love
- myrtle: undying love, peace
- naked figure: truth, purity, innocence
- oak: strength of faith and virtue, endurance, hospitality
- olive branch: peace, forgiveness, humanity, harmony
- open gates: after life, the soul entering heaven, entrance to heaven

- orb: faith
- owl: wisdom
- pall: mortality, mourning
- pansy: remembrance, meditation
- passion flower: Christ, of Christ's Passion, the Crucifixion, salvation from sin through Christ's sacrifice
- peacock: resurrection
- pelican: piety, atonement
- peony: honor, love
- pheasant: beauty, good fortune
- phoenix: resurrection
- pick: death, mortality
- pillow: the deathbed
- pineapple: fertility, friendship, hospitality
- plow: farmer
- poinsettia: the birth of hope; the Nativity, the birth of Christ
- poppies: eternal sleep, resurrection, eternal life, enlightenment, spiritual attainment
- pyramid: light, strength
- rainbow: union, fulfillment of the promise of resurrection
- ripened fruit: nourishment of the soul
- rod or staff: comfort to the bereaved
- rooster: awakening, resurrection, courage, vigilance
- rope circle: eternity
- rose: victory, pride, triumphant love, purity
- scales: justice, temperance
- scallop shell: birth, baptism, resurrection, life everlasting, pilgrimage of life
- scarab: resurrection, transcendence
- scepter: fortitude
- scythe: death, cutting life short, the final harvest
- severed branch: mortality
- shamrock: Irish descent, the Holy Trinity
- shattered urn: old age
- sheaf of wheat: old age, fruitful life
- shepherd's crook: charity
- skeleton: death, life's brevity
- skull: transitory, nature of earthly life, penitence, mortality
- skull and crossbones: death, crucifixion

- skull, crowned: trouble over death
- sleeping cherub: innocence
- smoke: vanity, futility of seeking earthly glory
- snail: laziness, sin
- snake: encircled everlasting life in heaven
- spade: mortality, death
- spider web: human frailty
- star: divine guidance
- Star of David: unity, transformation
- steps (three-tiered): faith, hope, charity
- sun disc: winged spirituality, everlasting life
- sun, rising: renewed life, resurrection, dawn of new life
- sun, setting: death
- sun, shining: everlasting life
- swallow: motherhood spirit of children, consolation
- sword: military
- sword, broken: life cut short
- sword, inverted: relinquishment of power, victory
- sword, sheathed: temperance
- swords, crossed: life lost in battle
- thistle: Scottish descent, earthly sorrow, defiance
- torch: immortality, purification, truth, wisdom
- torch, inverted: life extinguished
- tower: strength
- tree: life, knowledge, the fall of man through sin, human fruition or frailty
- tree, sprouting: regeneration life everlasting
- tree stump: life interrupted
- tree trunk: brevity of life
- tree trunk, leaning: short interrupted life, mourning
- triangle: the Holy Trinity
- triqueta (thee interlocking circles or triangles): eternity, trinity
- trumpet: announcement of the resurrection or the soul's entrance into heaven
- tulip: emblem of charity, the declaration of love, honor
- urn: immortality, penitence, the death of the body and its return to dust
- violet: humility
- water: life, weeping

- wheat: body of Christ, bread of life
- wheel: cycle of life, enlightenment, spiritual power
- willow: mourning, grief, lamentation, sorrow
- winged face: effigy of the deceased soul, the soul in flight
- winged hourglass: fleetness of life, mortality
- winged skull: flight of the soul from mortal man
- wreath: victory
- wreath of roses: heavenly joy and bliss
- wreath on skull: victory of death over life
- yew: mourning
- yin and yang: circle harmony, balance, birth and death

Chronology of Monument and Statue Placements in the City

The information here is believed to be the first attempt to amass a chronology for the statues and monuments that help tell the story of Richmond's history. Unlike the discovery theme of the text, this appendix includes placements on Monument Avenue, at the Virginia Museum of Fine Arts and at the capitol building. It was compiled from the best of information available in the hopes that it could be expanded and improved by our readers.

1607	First Cross, Twelfth and Canal (replaced in 1907)
1796	*George Washington* by Houdon, capitol rotunda
1800s	*Three Graces*, Maymont
1812	Monumental Church, Broad Street
1824	the bell tower, Capitol Square
1834	Arnold's Picket marker, Mulberry Street and Grove Avenue
1850	George Washington equestrian statue, Capitol Square
circa 1850	Benjamin Franklin gasolier, White House of the Confederacy
1855	Patrick Henry, Thomas Jefferson and George Mason in Washington equestrian statue, Capitol Square
1860	Henry Clay, Capitol Square
1867	Andrew Lewis, John Marshall and Thomas Nelson in Washington equestrian statue, Capitol Square

1875	General Thomas J. "Stonewall" Jackson, Capitol Square
1890	Robert E. Lee, Monument Avenue
	Thomas Jefferson, Jefferson Hotel
1891	General Williams Carter Wickham, Monroe Park
1892	Howitzers statue, Harrison Street and Park Avenue
	A.P. Hill, Laburnum Avenue and Hermitage Road
1894	Confederate Soldiers and Sailors Monument, Libby Hill Park
1898	*Joy of Life*, Governor's Mansion
1901	*Jefferson Standing on the Liberty Bell*, east corridor at Library of Virginia
	Virginia Mourning Her Dead, Museum of the Confederacy
1903	operating room from Old Dominion Hospital, Twelfth and Broad Streets
1904	Dr. Hunter Holmes McGuire, Capitol Square
1905	Morgan Fountain, Shockoe Slip
1906	Governor William "Extra Billy" Smith, Capitol Square
1907	J.E.B. Stuart, Monument Avenue at Stuart Circle
	Jefferson Davis, Monument Avenue
1911	Joseph Bryan, Monroe Park
	Powhatan Stone, Chimborazo Park
1915	cannon, 2300 Monument Avenue between Davis and Allison Streets
1916	Triton Fountain, Virginia Museum of Fine Arts
1919	Thomas "Stonewall" Jackson, Monument Avenue at Boulevard
1925	Hotchkiss Field baseball monument, Brooklyn Park Boulevard
1926	Anna River Bridge abutment, 2800 block, Kensington Avenue
1927	Temperance Fountain, Bryd Park at the Roundhouse
	Columbus statue, Byrd Park, end of South Boulevard
1929	Virginia zero milestone, Capitol Square
	Matthew Fontaine Maury, Monument and Belmont Avenues
	Thomas "Stonewall" Jackson, Capitol Square
1930	First Regiment, Park and Stuart Streets at Lombardy Avenue
	Dooley sundial, Hampton Street opposite Maymont's main entrance
1932	carillon, Byrd Park end of Blanton Avenue
	George Washington marker, Monroe Park

1933	*Daphne*, Virginia Museum of Fine Arts
1938	cannon, 3400 Monument between Roseneath and Thompson Streets
1941	three bears grouping, VCU Medical Center Reception
	Benjamin Franklin gasolier, McGuire Building
1943	*La Riviere*, Virginia Museum of Fine Arts
1945	World War II Monument, Monroe Park
1947	World War II Monument, Maury Cemetery
1951	Statue of Liberty replica, Chimborazo Park
	Bianca 1951, Virginia Museum of Fine Arts
1954	*Reclining Figure*, Virginia Museum of Fine Arts
1955	Fitzhugh Lee, Monroe Park
	Memory, Virginia War Memorial
1957	Thomas Jefferson on Jefferson Building (formerly Blanton Building), Bank Street
1959	Edgar Allan Poe, Capitol Square
1962	*Working Model for Locking Piece*, Virginia Museum of Fine Arts
1966	*Oracle*, Virginia Museum of Fine Arts
1969	*Rotating Sphere*, Virginia Museum of Fine Arts
1973	*Bojangles*, Adams and Leigh Streets
1974	*Future*, Twelfth and Main Streets
1976	Harry Flood Byrd, Capitol Square
1978	dancing man statue, Bellevue School, 2301 East Grace Street
	Richmond Light Infantry Blues, Festival Park at Richmond Coliseum
	Sounding Pierce, 700 Byrd Street at Federal Reserve Bank
1982	*Arches with Columns*, Virginia Museum of Fine Arts
	Conductor, Virginia Museum of Fine Arts
1983	*Connecticut*, Lucky Strike Building, 2700 East Cary Street
	Vigil, McGuire Hospital
	Wheels, Brown's Island

1985	Hippocrates plaque, VCU Medical Center near Egyptian Building
	Quadrature, Tenth and Main streets
	Corporate Presence, Ninth and East Cary Streets
	Mr. Smedley, temporarily removed, in storage
1986	*Winds Up*, Ninth and Cary Streets
1987	*Remembrance*, south lawn of Cathedral of the Sacred Heart
	police memorial, Festival Park at Richmond Coliseum
	Gilbert Robertson Memorial Stone, Kensington Avenue and Boulevard
	Boatsman Tower, Tenth and Cary Streets
1992	*Headman*, Brown's Island
1993	*Park Guardian*, Belvidere and Idlewood Streets
	Boy on Stilts, VCU's Malbon Garden
1995	Nina Abady plaque, Festival Park at Richmond Coliseum
1996	*River of Tears*, New City Hall, Broad and Eighth Streets
	Arthur Ashe, Monument Avenue and Roseneath Road
	St. Philip arch, Egyptian Building courtyard
1997	*Relaxing at Shields Lake* (removed), Byrd Park
	War Horse, Virginia Historical Society
	In Pursuit of Growth and Achievement, Oliver Hill Courthouse
1998	"Mongo's Stone," Libby Hill Park
1999	*Archenima*, Pine Camp Park
2000	*Sunday*, Oliver Hill Detention Center
2001	*Follow the Leader (Children at Play)*, Maymont, Spottswood Avenue entrance
	Cradle, Richmond Ambulatory Authority at Hermitage Road and Overbrook Avenue
2003	*Kugel*, Science Museum of Virginia
	Lincoln and son statue, Tredegar Iron Works

	World War I Memorial flagpole, Byrd Park
	Skyrider, Main Street Station
	Viktoria's Station, Main Street Station
2005	*Thin Blue Line*, Richmond Police Headquarters, 200 West Grace Street
	statue of the shriner holding the child, Hermitage Road
2006	bears grouping, Maymont
2007	Slavery Reconciliation Statue *Triangle*, Fifteenth and Main Streets
	Box Brown, Canal Walk at Dock Street
2008	Virginia Civil Rights Memorial, Capitol Square
	Tableith, Franklin Street at VCU Monroe Park Campus
	Truth and Beauty, Franklin Street at VCU Monroe Park Campus
	Carl William Armstrong Memorial, Canal Walk
2009	*Beacon*, Police Fourth Precinct, 2900 Chamberlayne Avenue
	Movieland, the Boulevard
	Eugene Trani, in building at Cary and Cherry Streets
2010	*Bud and Seed Group*, Canal Walk on Dock Street
2011	*Deepwater Sponger*, Rockett's Landing
2012	Thomas Jefferson, Capitol Square
	Mill, Brown's Island

The City of Richmond's Public Art Program

HISTORY OF RICHMOND'S PUBLIC ART PROGRAM

In 1991, the Planning Commission, on the recommendation of the city council, appointed a Public Art Commission, putting into action a policy that had been in the planning stages since 1989. Representatives from a broad cross-section of citizens worked together to address the need to enrich the city's visual image with fine art, making it a more attractive place to live and a dynamic attraction for tourists. Since then, the Public Art Program (PAP), operating from within the Department of Community Development and financed with 1 percent of the budget of eligible city construction projects, has produced permanently installed works at sites throughout the city.

THE PURPOSE OF THE PUBLIC ART PROGRAM IN RICHMOND

Recognizing that art in public places enriches the social and physical environment and provides experiences that enable people to better understand and appreciate their community and individual lives, the Public Art Commission's goal is to encourage an empowering sense of ownership and pride in community-shared public spaces. By ensuring the inclusion of the highest-quality art in public buildings and facilities throughout the city and encouraging the participation of the surrounding communities in various stages of the artworks' development, Richmond's Public Art Program is directly involved in building the social fabric of the city.

How the Public Art Program Works

Based on national models initiated up to twenty years ago (and passed into law in twenty-seven states and nearly two hundred municipalities), Richmond's Public Art Program follows well-established guidelines, adapted to our particular needs. A 1 percent allocation for art is earmarked from the city's capital budget from appropriate new or renovation construction projects having budgets of more than $250,000. "Appropriate" projects are ones that provide public services and accessibility, such as firehouses, police precincts, courthouses and detention centers, hospitals, clinics, passenger terminals, parks and recreation centers. The PAP also has a "gifts" policy to review, accept and place donated works of art to the city.

The 1 Percent for Art Process

All forms of visual art, conceived in any medium, may be commissioned or purchased. For each project, a site selection team is convened consisting of representatives of the "users" of the facility, members of the community, the architect, a city official (usually from the sponsoring city agency) and two to three members of the Public Art Commission, one of whom is an artist. Through an open call to artists (distributed regionally by direct mail and, for selected projects, advertised nationally through print media), applications are reviewed for artistic quality and appropriateness of their ideas or concepts to the specific project. The site requirements and the nature of the community are seriously considered when the selection team makes its recommendations. The artist may be asked to conduct workshop sessions with the representatives of the community to ensure the artwork's eventual acceptance. The process of work and the adherence to the timeline is monitored by the program's coordinator, and payments are allocated at appropriate intervals of completion. Included in the budget is an appropriation for maintenance and restoration.

There is no art set aside for infrastructure projects—such as rewiring a building or laying pipe underground—that are not visible to the public.

Although formal public meetings are not held, citizens wishing to have input can get on the meeting agenda; the meetings are held every second Tuesday of the month in the fifth-floor conference room of city hall at 9:15 a.m.

Present members of the commission include:

- Susan Reed, Chair—architect representative
- William Hutchins—planning commission member
- Mark Olinger—director, Department and Development Review
- Paul DiPasquale—sculptor, Culture Works representative
- Sarah Shields Diggs—Urban Design Committee
- Holly Morrison—Visual Arts
- Francis Thompson—Visual Arts Education
- Mr. Jerry (Jay) Sharpe Jr.—Visual Arts

Three vacancies exist at this time.

Each member serves a three-year term. All are required to attend meetings; any one missing three consecutive meetings or four in a year is automatically dismissed from the commission.

Vacancies are filled by sitting members, subject to approval by the city's Planning Commission, which oversees the Public Art Commission and ratifies its recommendations for the purchase of artwork.

The process may be better understood by an actual example. Following are the details of the bids for City of Richmond Fire Station No. 17, located at 2211 Semmes Avenue.

CITY OF RICHMOND FIRE STATION NO. 17

The City of Richmond Public Art Commission is seeking qualified artists to create commissioned outdoor artwork for the Springhill District and Community. The selected site is located on the grounds of under construction Fire Station No. 17 along Richmond's Semmes Avenue. The total purchase budget for this project is $27,000.

PROJECT BACKGROUND

Construction began in fall of 2011 to replace the old and outdated Fire Station No. 17 with a more modern facility with easier access. Plans are attached.

PROJECT DESCRIPTION

This Call for Artists requests proposals for original artwork created specifically for Fire Station No. 17. No previously created or designed artwork will be considered. The artwork should strengthen the identity of this facility and should create a sense of place for both employees and passers-by on the busy thoroughfare. Themes should respect the building's purpose, but need not be limited to fire fighting. The artwork should be extremely durable. The site for artwork will be in back of the station in the lawn area between the building and Canoe Run Park. Other locations around the building can be considered. Specific sites will be discussed at the pre-submission meeting and tour of the site.

REVIEW PROCESS

The Site Selection Team, made up of members of the Public Art Commission, the landscape architect, and City official, will review all complete proposals and choose finalists. Finalists will be selected based upon their previous work and their specific proposals. Each finalist will then be asked to create, and present in person, a specific proposal for review. An honorarium will be paid to each finalist upon successful submission of their proposal. The selected proposal(s) will then be recommended to the Public Art Commission and the City Planning Commission for review and approval. Once approved, the City will enter into a contract with the selected artist(s). If no proposals are deemed suitable, the Public Art Commission reserves the right to reopen the search for artists and/or take whatever action deemed appropriate to complete the selection process.

ELIGIBILITY

The City of Richmond's Public Art Program is open to all professional artists, regardless of race, gender, age, belief, or national origin. While artists from the Richmond metropolitan area are encouraged to participate, *there are no geographic boundaries affecting eligibility or selection. The primary criteria will be: a) the level of expertise and quality in conception and fabrication of art work as demonstrated by the materials submitted, b) the suitability of artist's work to context and placement on the building or on site and c) the artist's statement. Released Feb. 23, 2012. See printed ordinance.*

SUBMISSION REQUIREMENTS

All material should be submitted on a PC compatible CD-ROM, and three copies should be submitted. Each CD-ROM should include:

- *A maximum of twelve digital images of no more than six original works may be submitted—six works and up to six detail images. The digital images must be formatted as follows: jpeg format, up to 200 dpi, maximum 600 x 800 pixels. Label all images with your name and image number (e.g., smith1.jpg, smith2.jpg). Please number the images in the order in which you would like them shown.*
- *Please provide corresponding image numbers for the digital files submitted. Indicate the title of each work, date, media and dimensions. Include your name, mail and email addresses, phone and fax numbers, your website and online photo gallery at the top of this sheet.*
- *An artist résumé with art and public art commissions.*
- *A letter of interest/approach, not to exceed one page in length. This should not be a detailed project description, but rather a general statement of intent or approach. You may include up to three drawings.*
- *A maximum of three pieces of support material, such as exhibition announcements, reviews or newspaper clippings. Do not send originals, as this material will be retained along with your résumé.*
- *A completed application form.*

Note: An artist may submit more than one project. However, a complete application will be required for each proposal.

PRE-SUBMISSION MEETING AND TOUR

There will be a pre-submission meeting on Thursday, March 29, 2012, at 5:30 p.m. at the site of the station at 2211 Semmes Avenue in Richmond, Virginia. City staff, the landscape architect and members of the Site Selection Team will be present to answer questions about possible art locations, submission requirements and the selection process and criteria. Artists are strongly encouraged to attend this meeting. The Public Art Commission staff is also available by phone at (804) 646-3709 or by e-mail at jonathan.baliles@richmondgov.com to answer questions.

Note: A bill was introduced on January 4, 2012, to limit the amount for each qualifying project to $250,000 and change references of the city manager to chief administrator. No action was taken at time of publication of this report.

Potential Additions to the Monuments in Richmond

As time goes on, individuals and organizations propose ideas for new statues to commemorate heroes and events of the past. Who would like to add nominees to the list below?

William Byrd
James Branch Cabel
Emily Clarke
Virginius Dabney
Jimmy Dean
Sarah Shields Diggs
Douglas Southhall Freeman
Paul Galanti
Phyllis Galanti
Ellen Glasgow
Mills Godwin
Bruce Heilman

Shirley MacLaine
Jeff McNeeley
Lewis Powell
Dr. Ferguson Reid
Sally Tompkins
Laura Mead Valentine
Virginia Native Americans
Maggie Walker
Douglas Wilder
Michael Paul Williams
Tom Wolfe

Virginia Sculptors

REFLECTIONS ON A SCULPTOR

Looking at a large block of stone, how many of us can see an image inside, as Michelangelo is said to have observed? Even if you get over the initial vision hurtle, it's only the beginning. Chipping away the excessive stone is the hard part. One false move with the hammer can foil the whole project.

Another way of getting to the desired result may necessitate casting pieces separately to be assembled over a structural armature. Typically, this is not a one-person job. Depending on the size of the work and the difficulties encountered, or when working with certain media, the job cannot be finished without the assistance of other talented individuals with an understanding of the technical procedures.

The casting process is a good example of how others get involved. This has to be part of the repertoire, and it can be a complicated process. All bronze castings are actually hollow "skins" of bronze, often less than half an inch in thickness. It takes the skill of a foundry to make the hollowed impression of the original sculptor's model into the body of a mould.

This mould must contain the impressions of the surface of the original, as well as the tubes and channels needed to distribute the molten bronze to all the different parts of the impression. Knowing how to handle the composition is an important aspect of the procedure. However accomplished, the sculptor must be the jack-of-all-trades at the near-genius level.

Chiseling the stone or finding a dependable foundry can be challenging. It often comes after the artist has been involved in the fundraising process and/or experienced legal negotiation with the one who commissioned the work and is providing the financing. Insurance policies are often required on the sculptor and the key foundry man to ensure completion in the event of disability or death of either before delivery.

Historically, sculpture did not become a profession in America until the mid-1800s. In the early days, most sculptors had to study abroad, often traveling to Italy and France, where qualified instruction was plentiful. Following the Centennial Exposition of 1876, a new natural pictorial style emerged, influenced by the development of photography. By the end of the nineteenth century, complex bronze compositions in the French style predominated, and American art moved toward sentiment and realism.

As the demand rose for statues and memorials to commemorate the founders, heroes and events of the United States, Richmond artists were quick to meet the need, and a cadre of talented individuals turned out a variety of outstanding work. A brief résumé of some of these individuals follows. The list has been restricted to those who were either Virginia born or Richmond citizens who placed statues in our city.

WILLIAM L. COUPER (1853–1942)

Couper was born in Norfolk, Virginia. He developed an interest in sculpture watching Italian craftsmen carving marble in his father's business, the Couper Marble Works.

Couper's early training was in Munich and Florence. He was sponsored by noted Richmond sculptor Edward V. Valentine. Upon his return to the United States, Couper first established himself in New York in 1897 as a portraitist and sculptor of busts in the modern Italian style. He also completed dignified portrayals of military heroes, historical figures, public figures and allegorical figures representing literary and moral subjects as seen in numerous public places, institutions and museums.

Couper became a colleague of Daniel Chester French and went on to mold the Richmond statues of Hunter McGuire (1904), Joseph Bryan (1907) and Captain John Smith at Jamestown (1909).

PAUL DIPASQUALE (1952–)

DiPasquale got his start in Perth Amboy, New Jersey (June 15, 1952). A quick learner, he graduated first from the University of Virginia with distinction in sociology and a minor in art. He continued his studies and earned a master's degree with honors at Virginia Commonwealth University in 1977.

DiPasquale produces sculpture about history and the people who make it. He somehow finds time to be active in his neighborhood civic association and has been a board member of arts commissions and museum and service organizations. Since 1978, he has taught college courses in Virginia, Maryland and Washington, D.C.

In 1996 and 1998, DiPasquale was awarded a visiting artist position at the American Academy in Rome. Locally, he has contracted with and won awards and grants from the Virginia Museum of Fine Arts, the Children's Museum, the Commission for the Arts, the Arts Council of Richmond and the city and tri-county school systems.

Paul DiPasquale is listed in *Who's Who in the World* and *Who's Who in America* and has been published in leading publications across the globe. Richmond voted him Richmonder of the Year for his roles as author, producer and sculptor in 1996.

His placements are found at the Smithsonian's National Air and Space Museum, the Baltimore Aquarium, the Billings Rockefeller Museum in Vermont and at numerous corporations. The variety of collections nationally attests to his versatility and outstanding talent.

His *Peeking Ducks*, a copyright line of ceiling and wall duck and fish sculptures, has been sold nationally since 1988. Also included among his vast repertoire are these Richmond installations: *Connecticut, Headman* and depictions of Arthur Ashe, Oliver Hill and Mary McClanahan.

DONALD EARLEY

The creation of the moving statue in city hall, *River of Tears*, is the work of Donald Earley, his only bronze. He also completed a glass commission for actor Eli Wallach. In addition to the bronze and glass pieces, Earley has demonstrated his ability in a variety of artistic areas, including painting, drawing, etching, drypoint, sketching and lithography.

Earley holds a BA from the Fashion Institute of Technology in New York City, where he later joined the faculty before becoming affiliated with VCU in 1984. He is currently a professor in the fashion department of Virginia Commonwealth University's Doha, Qatar campus, where he teaches drawing, illustrating and exhibits. His work in that field of fine art has received recognition in shows nationwide.

Adding to his versatility, Earley will be included in a folktale book entitled *The Donkey Lady and Other Tales from the Gulf* to be published in 2013 by Berkshire Press. His accomplishments are best summed up by a quote from the artist: "When I look at my work, I feel like I am living on the edge of life holding a butterfly net trying to catch dreams as they go by—I am a romantic."

MOSES EZEKIEL (1844–1917)

Ezekiel was born in Richmond and attended public schools. He went on to graduate from the Virginia Military Institute in 1866 as the first Jewish cadet to accomplish that feat. Ezekiel was a highly decorated Confederate soldier in the Civil War. He and other cadets marched eighty miles to fight in the 1864 Battle of New Market, where he was wounded.

Following the war, with the memory of six cadets killed in this conflict still fresh in his mind, he went on to be admitted into the Society of Artists in Berlin and at age twenty-nine was the first foreigner to win the Michel-Beer Prix de Rome.

Ezekiel continued to receive numerous honors, including being recognized by the king of Italy, the emperor of Germany and the prince of Saxe-Meiningen and being knighted by the monarch of England.

Richmond has replicas of two of his finest works: *Virginia Mourning Her Dead* (1903) at the White House of the Confederacy and *Jefferson Standing on the Liberty Bell* (1901) at the Library of Virginia.

Despite his outstanding accomplishments and many honors, Ezekiel is often remembered by commentators quoting the modest inscription on his tombstone at Arlington National Cemetery:

Moses J. Ezekiel
Sergeant of Company C
Battalion of Cadets of the
Virginia Military Institute

LINDA GISSEN

A former Richmond resident, Gissen now lives in Virginia Beach. Ms. Gissen is a graduate of the University of Cincinnati and studied at the University of Michigan. Her studies include ethnic art and indigenous cultures in forty countries, and she has done extensive research on the Torah. Ms. Gissen specializes in art symbolizing stories from the Bible. Lessons of faith, strength and persistence flow from her creations.

Once a painter, Gissen became fascinated by the effects of heat on color—the way vitreous glazes would melt onto metal surfaces. Upon learning welding and later glassblowing, she never returned to the canvas. Read about one of her finest works, *Remembrance*, in the "Downtown" chapter.

A 1987 exhibit of her work was a very prestigious one-person show held at the House of Living Judaism on Fifth Avenue in New York. On this occasion, Ms. Gissen displayed her series of sculptures of women from scripture. The series was done in memory of her mother.

Her work continues. "I'm constantly discovering new possibilities," she enthusiastically stated in a *Richmond Times-Dispatch* report in 1998.

JAMES HUBARD (1807–1862)

James Hubard was born in Warwick, England. He arrived in the United States in 1824 as an internationally known silhouettist. The following year, he had an exhibition demonstrating his ability with scissors. His repertoire of groups of animals, landscape scenery, caricatures and so on was enthusiastically received and lauded in the press.

He later married and started another career as a painter. Encouraged by such greats as Gilbert Stuart and Thomas Sully, and after three years' study in Italy and France, he enjoyed success in this endeavor as well. Some of his work can be seen in the Valentine Museum collection.

Ever ambitious, Hubard continued to take on new challenges. He built a factory and was granted permission to replicate the famous Houdon marble statue of George Washington in bronze. After three failures, he produced six in 1856.

Having the foundry and always seeking to broaden his talents, Hubard decided to produce ammunition for the Brookings Gun. This would prove to be his last expansion, as in February 1862, Hubard was killed in an accidental explosion at the foundry.

FERRUCCIO LEGNAIOLI

Ferruccio Legnaioli studied in Paris, Florence and New York before coming to Richmond in 1907 after working on the decorations on several buildings at the University of Virginia. While in the city, he is credited with the Columbus statue just outside Byrd Park, the First Regiment statue ("Military" chapter) at Park and Stuart Streets, the horse fountain ("Downtown" chapter) in Shockoe Slip and the zero mile marker at the capitol.

Legnaioli also designed the seal over the north entrance to city hall and the plaster ornamentation for the Empire, National, Byrd and Colonial Theaters.

CHARLES PONTICELLO (1956–)

Ponticello is not only a graduate of VCU's School of Sculpture (BFA degree, 1989) but also a supporting alumni. His son, Andre, received his BFA from the same institution before going on to earn an MFA from Tyler School of Art. His daughter, Myiad, also enrolled to earn her BFA. In Ponticello's words, "Be hard for me to get away from VCU." His *Taleith* sculpture celebrating VCU's fortieth anniversary is a big hit on the VCU campus.

During the last several years, Ponticello has been on a crusade through his sculpture to bring attention to global warming and its repercussions. His emphasis has been on projects related to fresh water awareness. His

"Sponger" series is used to highlight the potential water problems of the day. *Deepwater Sponger* (at Rockett's) and the *Deviner* display (at Red Door Gallery) are already complete and in place. Watch for *The Engineer* to be added to the series in 2013.

Leon Reid IV (1979–)

Reid, also known as Verbs and Darius Jones, born in Richmond, is an American artist widely credited as being among the pioneers of twenty-first-century "street art." Reid holds degrees from Pratt Institute and Central Saint Martins School of Art and Design. His creativity is not disputed, but his work is often controversial.

Reid now works out of Brooklyn, New York, after living in Cincinnati and London. He claims to have installed more than 150 pieces in Brooklyn and Manhattan.

Bradley Robinson (1964–)

Bradley Robinson trained as a decorative blacksmith near Washington, D.C., and has carried out commissions for several national institutions, including the Washington National Cathedral, Rice University and Washington and Lee University. He has worked on many significant residential projects featured in *Architectural Digest, Traditional Home* and *Home & Design* magazines. He also participated in the documentary *Masters of the Building Arts* by Oscar-winning filmmakers Marjorie Hunt and Paul Wagner.

Since setting up a studio in Richmond in 2006, Bradley has turned his attention to contemporary sculpture and recently completed traveling studies to England and France. He is preparing for his first exhibition in 2013 at Page Bond Gallery in Richmond. His recent statue creation, *Mill*, was placed on Brown's Island and has been well received.

Allan Rosenbaum

Rosenbaum earned a BS at the University of Wisconsin in 1978 and continued his training, receiving an MFA in 1986 from Virginia Commonwealth University, where he remained to teach following his graduation.

Mr. Rosenbaum left his first love—humorous, narrative figurative sculptures and sculpture teapots—to complete the highly regarded bronze statue *Cradle*, displayed at the Richmond Ambulatory Authority headquarters, located at the intersection of Hermitage and Overbrook Roads.

The seriousness of the work is in contrast to his ceramic creations, which he explained as follows:

> *My work negotiates a balance between the real and the imaginary—between our daily experiences and our dreams. The sculptures I make weave together objects and images that are culled from personal memories, art history, domestic interiors and urban environments. By creating sculptures that are composed of combinations of familiar images, I hope to shed new light on the metaphorical possibilities of the figure and of the objects in our everyday world. Through my work, I raise questions about the nature of human relationships, the need for security, our methods of communication, the search for identity and the importance of community.*

This may explain how he was able to send a message in a new medium.

William Ludwell Sheppard (1833–1912)

Sheppard was born in Richmond on August 31, 1833. After employment and study in New York, he traveled to Paris for additional training. He eventually returned to Richmond to join the Confederate army in 1861 and served four years with the Richmond Howitzers.

The war provided Sheppard with an endless source of subject matter for sketching, which he later used as reference material for watercolor, wash and pen and ink renderings of Confederate life.

After the war, Sheppard began a prolific artistic career, ever expanding his media. His paintings gained him national recognition, appearing in several popular magazines of the day. Sheppard painted or copied paintings in the U.S. Capitol of Culpeper, Lord Drummond, Richard Henry Lee, Lord Howard, Thomas Lee, Nicholas, Pendleton and Percy. Several of his paintings are held by the Valentine History Museum, and his statue designs are placed throughout the city.

The Confederate Soldiers and Sailors Monument on Libby Hill (1894), the Howitzer at Harrison and Park (1892), A.P. Hill on Hermitage Road (1892) and Governor Billy Smith at the capitol (1907) attest to his outstanding talent and versatility.

FREDERIC WILLIAM SIEVERS (1872–1966)

Sievers studied at the Royal Academy of Fine Arts in Rome and the Académie Julian in Paris. He moved to Richmond when he was commissioned to create the Virginia monument in Gettysburg, Pennsylvania. Sievers maintained his residence and studio in what is now 1206 West Forty-third Street for more than half a century. Here he became one of the South's most prolific sculptors. The acceptance of his work is evident in the widespread distribution of his statues throughout the South and beyond.

His popularity led to several other Civil War sculptures, including two Monument Avenue statues: General Stonewall Jackson in 1919 and Matthew Fontaine Maury in 1929. His contribution to Richmond also includes four portrait statues at the capitol: Presidents James Madison and Zachary Taylor and two others, Patrick Henry and Sam Houston.

Sievers is buried at Forest Lawn Cemetery, and a historical marker commemorates his workshop on West Forty-third Street.

WILLIAM TURNER (1935–) AND DAVID TURNER (1961–)

This father/son team of William and David Turner operates the largest bronze foundry in the United States. Their work appears in hundreds of museums, universities, art galleries, corporations and fine homes throughout the nation and in several countries abroad.

The senior Turner is a graduate of the VCU School of Dentistry. He actually practiced dentistry before putting his talents as an architect, builder, carver and sculptor to work to form the present company in 1983. He also found time to write three books with themes built around the rural life that surrounds their company.

The Turners share their talents capturing the beauty and motion of wildlife in bronze. This has resulted in more than four hundred different limited-edition creations and more than fifty large public commissions. Inspirations for their creations originate from their native land, the Eastern Shore of Virginia, a peninsula surrounded by the Chesapeake Bay and Atlantic Ocean. Showing their versatility, *Boy on Stilts* at VCU stands out as an exception.

EDWARD VALENTINE (1838–1930)

Valentine was born and died in Richmond. In between, he studied in Europe under Couture and Jouffroy in Paris, under Bonati in Italy and under August Kiss in Berlin.

In a career spanning fifty years, Valentine worked in clay, plaster, marble and bronze to produce a variety of sculptures. First specializing in portrait sculpture, he eventually went on to create hundreds of pieces. The Valentine Richmond History Center Museum, for which he was the first president, holds 350 of his plaster moulds together with his furniture, papers, tools and memorabilia. The accumulation is one of only four nineteenth-century sculptor studios in the United States open to the public, offering a rare opportunity to view a large collection of original artwork in a setting in which it was created, along with the sculptor's tools and other personal effects included.

Valentine's finest work may be the Robert E. Lee sculpture that he produced for the Lee Chapel at Washington and Lee University in Lexington, Virginia. Another of his renditions of Lee is one of Virginia's two allotted statues in the U.S. Capitol. Richmond is fortunate to have another of his best works: the statue of Thomas Jefferson at the hotel (1895) named for our third president.

The Wickham statue (1891), which replaced Richmond's Washington Monument in Monroe Park, and the magnificent presentation of Jefferson Davis (1907) on Monument Avenue are other examples of Valentine's talent and contribution to the city's collection.

Valentine was very active presenting other military commanders besides Lee. He included in his clientele such notable generals as Beauregard, Breckenbridge, Jackson, Johnson, Mahone, Mercer, Mosby, Pickett and Stuart.

On the civilian side, names like Poe, Mordecai, Audubon and Billy Smith augment his ability to work with the influential of the day.

LESTER VAN WINKLE

Lester Van Winkle was born and bred in east Texas. He received his master's degree from University of Kentucky and a BS from East Texas State University. His talent has been displayed from California to New York and in Europe. His sculptures are part of numerous public and private collections, and he has been the recipient of two NEA fellowships. His work may best be classified as figurative, either carved or cast or welded, of wood or aluminum or steel.

Professor Van Winkle could have easily made his mark on the strength of his art alone. Choosing to share his knowledge in the classroom was a fortunate decision for the Virginia Commonwealth University School of Sculpture. His long tenure (more than forty years) and ability to transfer his knowledge to the students has played a major role in building the program to the nation's number-one ranking among college schools of sculpture.

His accomplishments didn't come by accident. Van Winkle had rules to guide his students, and they quickly became familiar with "Lester's Laws":

1. *Do not arrive on time for this class. Be early and appear busy. Punctuality and thrift precede cleanliness in the eyes of "You Know Who."*

2. *Have ideas in your work. Mere personal expression is unavoidable, highly overrated and can be sloppily self-indulgent.*

3. *If you have no ideas, check your pulse.*

4. *If you have an idea (one), you are in trouble.*

5. *If you steal ideas, cover your tracks. Be the master thief. Do the perfect crime. Or don't be a postmodern, deconstructivist, conceptual appropriationist. Plagiarism is in fashion. Fashion is vicious and violent.*

6. *Remember that in our game an idea is no better than its articulation.*
7. *Speak up in critiques. Ye shall be known by your words.*
8. *In critiques do not say, "I like." For obvious reasons, like you're talking mostly about yourself or whatever.*
9. *If you believe that criticism is only personal opinion, quit school now. Save your money. Personal opinions are absolutely free and in infinite supply on the street.*
10. *Beware of art jargon. No one knows what words like "balance" and "rhythm" mean.*
11. *Believe me, there is nothing negative about space. The constructivists considered space a tangible material.*
12. *Never let your story be more interesting than your art.*
13. *Never explain your choices by what you did not want. What you did not want or intend is an infinite set.*
14. *Do not let American industry make the color, surface, image, proportional or scale choices in your work.*
15. *High-tech, avant-garde or expensive traditional materials will not improve bad ideas.*
16. *Simple repetition never doesn't work. Repetition, like contrast, is a visual phenomenon, not a conceptual issue.*
17. *Do not make things the same size without good reason.* MODERN REVISION: *No, do not make things the same size.*
18. *Do not center or divide things in the middle. The middle is such a swell place; it should always be reserved for special occasions.*
19. *Do not use obvious proportion ratios. 1:1, 2:1, 2:4 etc.*
20. *Avoid bilateral symmetry and 90 degree angles. (See special occasions.)*
21. *Do not arrange things that lead your eye in a circle, square, rectangle, triangle, cube, cone, etc.*
22. *If you want to use black, white or gray, see me first.*
23. *Always make primary colors secondary choices.*
24. *Give color significant jobs to do in your work.*
25. *Paint all carvings, particularly stone carvings.*
26. *Find significant terminations for three-dimensional lines.*
27. *Always radically modify or rectify found objects.*
28. *Remove source references from found objects.*
29. *Make weird things. It is an artist's job to do so.*
30. *Remember that all things in the same context relate. Any further similarities, connections, parallels, vectors or threads only compound an already existing relationship.*

31. The only thing worse than a bad piece of sculpture is a big, bad piece of sculpture. Even worse is a big, bad, red piece of sculpture.

32. Trust your instincts. Trust your intuition. They are your best tools.

Jack Witt

Jack Witt, author and sculptor, earned a BA in English from Virginia Military Institute and studied painting and drawing as apprentice to Eugene Califano in Taos, New Mexico. He later earned his MFA in sculpture from Virginia Commonwealth University.

Notable examples of his work include the Bill "Bojangles" Robinson monument in Richmond, the *Mr. Smedley* figure in Richmond and Lincoln at Lincoln Memorial University, Harrogate, Tennessee.

Roses are Red and White, Witt's collection of poetry, was published by Brandylane. He combined talents with wife Judy in two publications that emphasize the exquisite beauty in a region of Virginia: *Goshen and Lessons from the River: Writings, Watercolors, Drawings, Sculpture* and *Goshen Revisited*.

Mr. Witt resides in Ashland, Virginia.

Glossary

It comes naturally to admire the talent of the sculptor when viewing monuments and statues, but understanding the full message of his or her design is not always easy. So many forms, media and symbols make it difficult to absorb the full meaning. Just as music speaks an international language, statues and monuments have a way of communicating with people of all tongues.

This glossary includes definitions, sayings and proverbs relating to sculpture and makes it easier to comprehend the message of the artist—to see what you see. You may wish to review the symbolism section in Appendix I for further clarity.

abacus: the flat slab on the top of a capital.

abstract: any art in which the depiction of real objects in nature has been subordinated or entirely discarded and whose aesthetic content is expressed in a formal pattern or structure of shapes, lines and colors. Sometimes, the subject is real but stylized, blurred, repeated or broken down into basic forms as to be unrecognizable. Sculpture that is partly broken down in this way is called "semiabstract." When the representation of real objects is completely absent, as opposed to realistic or figurative sculpture, such art may also be called "nonrepresentational." An abstract element or intention appears in works of art and decoration throughout the history of art, from Neolithic stone carvings onward. Abstraction as an aesthetic principle began in the early twentieth century with Braque (1882–1963).

academic sculpture: following the traditions of style of an academy, often lacking in original concept by the sculptor.

acanthus: a prickly herb found in the Mediterranean region, the leaves of which were a principal decorative motif for furniture and architecture in classical times, such as the Corinthian capital; especially popular in the United States during the Greek Revival period (1815–50) and the Beaux Arts period (1880–1920).

acropodium: a classical term referring to a large pedestal for a statue, usually made of marble highly embellished with low-relief carvings.

acroterion: carved decorative device placed above the corners of a pediment on classical or Neoclassical buildings. It is usually pointed, for example in the shape of a pinnacle, but it can be in a form of plinths and statues or on the apex or at the ends of a pediment.

allegorical sculpture: symbolic representation of an idea or a principle.

ankh: a cross shaped like a "T" with a loop at the top, especially as used in ancient Egypt as a symbol of life.

apotheosis: in classical times, the elevation of a mortal to the rank of a god or the glorification of a person, principle or ideal.

arch: the spanning of an opening by reasons other than that of a lintel.

architecture: with relation to sculpture, any component of a building or structure that has been modeled, carved or welded by a sculptor and integrated into the whole in some manner so as to embellish or enhance it, as distinguished from work created for display independently. A caryatid is an example of this. The two subjects or art forms of sculpture and architecture have been closely related through the ages.

architrave: in classical architecture, that part of the entablature resting immediately above the capitals of columns and supporting the frieze.

archivolts: bands or mouldings surrounding an arched opening.

armature: a bracing; a construction made of wood, light or heavy metal wire, bars or piping or other suitably rigid material to support the wet clay, wet plaster or other soft and pliable mixed media materials used by a sculptor to model or construct a sculpture.

armillary sphere: an early astronomical instrument composed of bronze rings representing the positions of the principal circles of the celestial spheres.

art: 1. the making or doing (hence the terms "maker," "creator" and "artist") by people or things that have form and beauty. Sculpture, painting, architecture, music, literature, poetry, drama, dance and cinema are some of the forms of art. 2. the actual sculptures, drawings, paintings or films made by artists. 3. any of certain areas of learning as philosophy, sculpture, music and so on, usually plural "arts." 4. the ability to make or do things; skill ("the art of cooking"). 5. any craft or special knowledge ("the art of healing"). 6. a sly or cunning trick; wile ("the arts of a successful politician").

Art Deco: a term that originated in circa 1960 referring to the style used in art and architecture between World War I and World War II. The name was taken from the Exhibitions of Decorative and Industrial Arts hosted by Paris in 1925. The style consists of streamlined lines, geometric patterns, boldness and simplicity, as well as the popular use of aluminum as a medium for sculpture; often referred to as Art Monerne at the time.

"art for art's sake": when you proclaim the independence of aesthetic values intrinsic in a work of art from storytelling, moral values or any other purposes or motives. From the French "l'art pour l'art."

artist's proof: one of the first verifications in a limited edition of original sculptures. Must bear the artist's signature or mark and, since the early twentieth century, is usually numbered. On a sculpture, the appropriate mark is "A/P."

art nouveau: a term referring to the style used in art and architecture during the period of 1880–1910 that was a reaction against academic traditions in art and the various decorative revivals that had been dominant for one hundred years; the principal feature consisted of the curved, slender, elegant line, with the most popular motif employed being the lily plant, especially in France.

assembly: one of the four main methods a sculptor may use to achieve a desired overall form. Basically, constructing or adding existing shapes, objects or materials to one another in a method other than welding to create a whole sculpture. See also **carving**, **modeling** and **welding**.

atlantes: the plural form of **atlas**; figures or half-figures of a human male used as columns to support a building or entablature.

atlas: the figure or half-figure of a human male used as a column to support a building or entablature. Atlas, one of the Titans (a family of giants in Greek mythology), was defeated by Zeus after a long battle. The Titans, consequently, were harshly punished, especially Atlas, who was forced to hold up the heavens with his arms for eternity; the plural form is **atlantes**.

Aztec: an ancient Indian tribe that wandered into Mexico in the fourteenth century and founded a highly developed civilization before the arrival of Columbus. This civilization was largely destroyed by Spanish rule under Hernán Cortés in the sixteenth century.

Baroque: a style developed in sculpture, architecture and art in the late Renaissance in reaction against the severity of classical form, employing great use of elaborate scrolls, curves and carved ornament.

base: also called a plinth. The base is what the sculpture is attached to, fixed to or mounted on; a block of any shape or dimension and material placed between a sculpture and its pedestal. These terms can all be confused, as a pedestal is also defined as a base or foundation.

bas-relief: French for "low relief" (*basso-rilievo* in Italian). In a bas-relief, the figures project only slightly, and no part is entirely detached from the background (as in medals and coins, in which the chief effect is produced by the play of light and shadow). See also **relief** and **haut-relief.**

***beaux-arts*/Beaux Arts**: French for "fine arts." The approach was originated in circa 1870 in the École des Beaux-Arts (National Academy of Fine Arts) in Paris. It wasn't received with any exuberance in the United States until after its introduction at the World's Columbian Exposition in Chicago in 1893. Its influence was felt as late as 1930.

bronze: an alloy of copper and tin, sometimes containing small amounts of other elements in varying proportions such as zinc and phosphorus. It is harder and more durable than brass and has been used extensively since antiquity for casting sculpture. Bronze alloys vary in color from silvery hues to rich, coppery reds. Different countries have different standards for the mix, and mixes also may vary from one foundry to another. In its molten form, bronze is poured into the main channel, or spruce, of an investment casing surrounding a sculpture to produce the final cast piece of artwork.

bust: a piece of sculpture representing the upper part of the human figure, including the head and neck and usually the upper section of the shoulders and chest, mounted on a base; often referred to as a "portrait bust."

Byzantine: of architecture of the Byzantine empire, developed during the fifth and sixth centuries; principle features include a doe carried on pedantries over a square, richly colored mosaics, marble veneering and often capitals carved in an endless variety of design with flat, low-relief carvings; the style originated in what is now Turkey.

caduceus: a staff used by a herald or messenger in ancient Greece, decorated with the two serpents coiled about it, with two wings at the top; associated with speed and healing and, in the United States, used as a symbol for communication offices, postal services and the medical profession.

calipers: a devise with two moveable jaws, used by sculptors to take measurements in the round while working; also used in making copies of original work. Calipers come in different sizes and are made of wood, brass, metal or plastic.

capital: the head or upper part of a column or pilaster, carrying the weight of the roof or entablature.

Carrara marble: a fine white marble mined in the mountains near Carrara, Italy, and having a flat rather than glossy surface when sculpted.

cartouche: an elaborate decorative panel with a border, frequently with a carved inscription or armorial seal; often found on architecture of the Baroque and Beaux Art periods.

carve: the process of taking away material from a given volume. In sculpture, it is the act of cutting or incising the material into the desired form using knives, chisels, gouges, points, saws, adzes and hammers. Today, modern artists often "rough out" their forms using electrically powered tools with care.

caryatid: in architectural sculpture, the female figure that serves as a column supporting an entablature. Usually a graceful figure dressed in long robes. From the Greek. Male counterparts are atlantes or tolomones.

cast: 1. to reproduce an object, such as a piece of clay sculpture, by means of a mould. Also, an artist may choose to cast from life-real objects or parts of a body or the entire body. This is often referred to as "moulage" or "life casting." 2. a copy produced by this means. The original piece is usually of a less durable material than the cast. See also **foundry** and **mould**.

casting: the process of making a mould (plaster or rubber, polymer and plaster and so on) from an original. Also, loosely, the activities that take place in the foundry. See **cast**.

cement: a building material made of lime, silica and alumina. Can be surface-colored or loaded with pigments for an all-through color and can be used to create outdoor sculptures. The sculptor will either cast his sculpture by pouring the cement into a mould made from an original piece in a softer material or work the cement onto a metal armature or other armature from suitably rigid material using a variety of tools. 2. Any strong adhesive used to join or repair materials, such as rubber cement or cellulose cement.

cheek block: a large block of marble or stone, carved or uncarved, used on the side of a flight of steps to support decorative sculpture, as an architectural device to support decorative sculpture or as an architectural device to support and balance the steps; often found in front of the porticos of classical and Neoclassical buildings and bridges.

cherub: a winged child, childlike angel or a child's head with wings, frequently found as a decorative motif for American cemetery sculpture during the second half of the nineteenth century and on American Beaux Arts buildings from 1890 to 1930.

classical: following the traditions, rules or styles of ancient Greece and Rome in sculpture, architecture and art.

clay: 1. a native earth consisting mainly of decomposed feldspathic rock containing kaolin and other hydrous aluminous minerals. Becomes hard when baked or fired. Used wet, it is then called "wet clay," as compared with what is often called "modeling clay." 2. sold under various names such as plasticine and lastilina; originally made in Italy with tallow, sulfur and high-quality clay. Also made less expensively with clay, an inert filler and various petroleum oils and greases heated and thoroughly mixed; can be variously colored (i.e., if made with graphite oil, it is blackish, and if made with normal car oil, it is yellow-green).

colonnade: a row of columns carrying an entablature or arches.

Columbia: female figure symbolic of the United States, similar to the Britannia of Great Britain.

column: an upright pillar or post.

corbel: a supporting architectural bracket or block projecting from a wall.

core: in sculpture/mould-making/casting terms, the core is the solid internal portion of an investment mould for casting a hollow piece of sculpture (such as a portrait). The amount of space left between the core and the mould (occupied by wax before it is lost) determines the thickness of the cast metal. The core is made of foundry sand (can also be same as investment material) in sand casting and in the lost-wax process.

Corinthian: the most ornate of the three ancient classical orders of architecture; characterized by columns surmounted by elaborate capitals, acanthus leaves and volutes, or scroll-like devices, at the corners.

cornice: the projecting horizontal part of the upper section of a building, frequently carved as an embellishment on classical and Neoclassical architecture.

cresting: the decorative work on the ridge of a roof, usually as a continuous series of finials, often using the acanthus leaf as a motif on classical and Neoclassical buildings.

crocket: a decorative ornament carved on the sloping edge of a gable or spire of a Gothic cathedral, often resembling bent foliage used on spires above flying buttresses.

cusp: curved, triangular-shaped projection from the inner curve of an arch or circle.

diagonal ribs: the mouldings that mark the diagonals in a rib vault in a tomb canopy.

diaper: a pattern formed by small, repeated geometrical motifs set adjacent to one another; used to decorate stone surfaces on monuments.

Doric: the oldest and simplest of the three ancient Greek orders of architecture, usually with fluted columns and plain rounded capitals.

edition: the making of replicas or copies of a sculptor's work.

exedra: a stone semicircular bench, usually in the open air, used in ancient Greece and frequently erected in the United States during the Beaux Arts period; often embellished with a statue in the center or low-relief carvings at the ends.

fasces: a bundle of rods bound by leather cords, with a projecting axe blade at the upper end, carried in processions in ancient Rome to symbolize the authority of the law; often found as a decorative device carved on Neoclassical buildings and used extensively on government property. The American counterpart traditionally does not use the axe.

faux: from the French for "false," said of any composite material made to look like another material or of a false finish given to a sculpture. "Faux marble" is usually reconstituted marble powder incorporated into resin, but it could also be a marble finish effect on, for example, a plaster cast.

figurative: of or portraying the figure (human or animal). Figurative sculpture can be either realistic (in varying degrees) or stylized.

firing: exposing to heat in a kiln a clay body to harden it or an investment casing containing wax so as to "lose it," which is an integral part of the lost-wax process.

foundry: the building or place where the casting of bronze takes place. Typically, a foundry will have subdivisions of activities taking place. The first step is making a mould or a negative container. Next, wax is poured into the moulds. After cleaning up the seams, a core is made, followed by spruing and gating the wax cast of the sculpture with wax strips or rods. This will ensure the smooth arrival of the molten metal into the negative space formed when the wax is "lost," encasing the entire piece into an investment. Then, "losing" the wax out of the invested piece by firing it, the molten bronze is poured into the main sprue, hacking away the investment material. Then they cut off the bronze sprues and gates, chasing away any other unwanted bronze (or filling in any holes). Chiseling and then either polishing or applying a patina and or wax to the sculpture completes the process. Mounting the final piece on a base is sometimes also an intricate part of the foundry's work.

frieze: a horizontal band that runs below the cornice. The frieze may be decorated with designs or carvings.

gate: in casting, any of the several channels or ducts through which molten material is carried from the main channel, or sprue, to the hollow part of the investment mould, or casing. The waste piece of material formed by such a duct is also called a gate and is removed from the cast metal along with the sprue as the first stage of cleaning up the sculpture. A gate is also sometimes called a "runner."

gesso: raised decoration made from calcium sulfate or calcium carbonate and animal glue.

griffin: a monster, often half-lion and half-eagle, used as a common decorative device in Greek and Roman art and sculpture; often symbolic of protection.

haut-relief: French for "high" or "deep" relief (*alto-rilievo* in Italian). In a haut-relief sculpture, the figures project at least half of their natural circumference from the background. See **relief** and **bas-relief**.

heroic: larger than life-size but smaller than colossal.

high-relief: sculpture or carving with great depth or with considerable projection from the background but not freestanding.

installations: a mode of work in which art elements (sculptural or otherwise) are installed in a location, either responding to the site itself (called "site-specific installation") or not.

interlace: a decorative motif consisting of threads passing over and under each other like threads in lace.

investment: a containing negative mould, used in sculpture for casting metals. It consists of either earth clay and sand or plaster of Paris mixed with clay, pulverized plaster asbestos fibers and glue size when mixed up for the lost-wax process. It is also sometimes called "casting."

Ionic: a capital used originally by the Greeks in a system of supports called the Ionic order. An Ionic capital has a volute, or a spiral scroll-like carving, on each side as its major decoration.

kinetic: pertaining to motion, especially to modern abstract sculpture that was designed by the sculptor to move through space.

laurel: the leaves of this tree were used by the ancient Greeks to crown the victors in athletic games and also as a mark of distinction for certain offices and functions; commonly used as a motif on cemetery sculpture for military officers in the United States during the second half of the nineteenth century.

limited: the set number of replicas or copies that a sculptor plans to make or has had made from an original, after which the mould is destroyed. The practice of limiting editions and numbering proofs originated with etchings and dry point, in which the quality of proofs declines as the copper plate begins to show signs of wear. By thus limiting the size of an edition to first-rate examples of a sculptor's work, the sculptor protects his or her artistic integrity and the value of the works to the collector. There is no technical reason for limiting or numbering editions of works of art that are made by processes capable of turning out an indefinite number of uniformly good copies, such as lithography or casting methods that employ durable moulds. And in any case, a new mould can be taken from the original to extend an edition. Editions are frequently limited, however, for financial reasons. By ensuring the relative rarity of the sculptor's work, he or she increases its value.

lost wax process: a technique for casting bronze sculpture in the United States during the nineteenth and twentieth centuries that consists of constructing a plaster model with a wax surface of suitable thickness. An outer mould covers the wax. When hot bronze is poured inside, the wax escapes, and a sculpture is formed in the empty space.

low-relief: bas-relief sculpture or carving with little depth or with slight projection from the background.

mandorla: an almond-shaped motif in which Christ sits. It is sometimes used also for the Virgin Mary.

marble: in its entire form, it is one of the hardest stones to carve. In fact, it is a hard type of limestone (more or less crystallized by metamorphism), often with streaks. It takes a high polish if desired. It is also one of the most expensive stones and therefore prized in its powdered form, which can be used to create bonded marble casts or "faux" marble as an alternative to plaster as a casting material. Resin can be loaded with marble powder, as can a cement mix.

medium: the material used for a given sculpture. Bronze, terra cotta, plaster and steel are all examples of media.

metal: 1. a chemical element that is more or less shiny and can be hammered, welded or stretched, such as iron, gold, aluminum, lead and magnesium. Distinguished from an alloy. In wire or wire mesh form (of varying dimensions), it can also be used to create sculpture. "Metalwork" is the term used to describe the making of things from metal. 2. glass in its molten state.

mixed media: when two or more media are used in a single work of art (e.g., metal and wood; metal, wood and stone, etc.). Mixed media include plastics, fibers and any man-made or natural element that can be used to model or otherwise construct a sculpture.

modal modeling: the very "forgiving," highly satisfying (physically and emotionally) process whereby a sculptor adds—bit by bit—wet clay or other soft medium such as wet plaster or cement or other media to build up or construct his or her original artwork, often using an armature. It is essentially an additive rather than a subtractive process, as contrasted with carving, though subtraction can also be and is often used in the process of achieving the desired shapes.

Monel: the trade name for a metal alloy of nickel and copper; has high resistance to corrosion.

mosaic: decoration created by setting small pieces of glass, stone or marble in a matrix. This was most popular for monuments in the Victorian period.

mould: a hollow or negative container used in the process of casting to give form to a substance placed within (wax for the bronze lost-wax process, plaster, cement, resin loaded or not with slate, marble, bronze powder and so on) and allowed to harden. Moulds can be made of plaster entirely or in rubber with an outer plaster jacket (also called "mother mould" or "casting").

A one-piece mould that must be destroyed to get the cast out is called a "waste mould." A mould consisting of two or more separable pieces is called a "piece mould." Often, a sculptor will see his finished bronze sculpture through the making of two such negative moulds either himself or at the foundry.

A first mould produces the mould in which the wax positive is poured. A second one is built in and around the positive and its sprue and gates, from which the wax is lost by firing in a kiln. This is hacked off to reveal the rough-cast bronze from which the sprue and gates will have to be removed. Metal casting is done by sand casting in which the negative containing a mould and a positive core—allowing the final piece to be hollow—are made of foundry sand.

nail head: an ornamental motif of small pyramids, said to represent the heads of nails, very popular in the twelfth century.

Neoclassical: pertaining to a revival of the art and architecture of ancient Greece and Rome, especially popular in the United States in the post–World War II era and later expanded to include American artists.

obelisk: a tall, tapering shaft of stone, usually monolithic, of a square or rectangle section and ending as a pyramid.

oculus: a circular opening in a canopy.

patina: a film or incrustation that forms on copper or bronze after a certain amount of weathering—the result of oxidation of the copper contained within bronze. When green, it is known as "aerugo" or "verdigris." Patinas are often made to occur in the foundry on the sculptor's request by special treatments that duplicate the green copper carbonates and hydrated oxides of natural bronze patinas.

Rarer bluish and reddish patinas can also be effected. A patina is normally a kind of protection that tends to retard further corrosion considerably. However, sometimes a malignant type of corrosion known as "bronze disease" occurs. The process whereby a patina is either naturally acquired or artificially induced is known as "pagination." Some sculptors imitate the pagination process on nonmetallic sculpture with the use of oils, waxes and pigments (e.g., shoe polish on plaster).

pedestal: 1a. the support or foot of a late classic or Neoclassic column. 1b. the base of an upright structure. 2. the base, foundation or support for a sculpture.

pediment: a low-pitched triangular gable on the front of a monument.

pendant: a hanging architectural member formed by ribs. They often appear in conjunction with fan vaults.

pilaster: a rectangular support that resembles a flat column. The pilaster projects only slightly from the wall and has a base, a shaft and a capital.

plinth: the base of a monument.

polychromy: the painted decoration applied to medieval stone tombs. The stone was initially sealed by a layer of size, perhaps animal glue; next, a thin layer of lead white was applied to form a ground. Finally, a thin layer of oil sealant was added to prevent absorption into the porous ground of binding media from subsequent paint layers and thus to ensure that the translucency of the polychromic was not compromised. The complex and sophisticated applied decoration involved—in addition to the layering of pigments—includes the use of raised decoration and gold and silver leaf beneath translucent glazes.

porphyry: a highly polished, finely textured hard stone, found in varying shades of red and green.

portrait: a portrait in sculpture comprising the head only or head and neck, as compared with a bust.

putti: nude children, wingless, used in decorative sculpture during the classical, Neoclassical and especially the Beaux Arts periods; chubby angel-like figures seen on post-Reformation monuments.

quatrefoil: an ornamental foliation having four lobes or foils, especially popular in the period of Gothic architecture and sculpture; decorative moulding often seen on tomb chests composed of four equal lobes, like a four-petal flower.

realistic: sculpture is dubbed realistic when it portrays real-life objects or people or recognizable, identifiable shapes. In general, the term is used for the depiction of human figures, real objects or scenes as they appear, without distortion or stylization (thus differentiated from that of figurative). It can also be used to mean representational or objective sculpture as distinguished from abstract sculpture.

relief: any work that projects from the background. Reliefs are classified by degree of projection. Relief sculpture is distinguished from sculpture in the round. No part is entirely detached from the background (as in medals, coins or areas of large reliefs in which the chief effect is produced by the play of light and shadow). In a haut-relief sculpture (high-relief or *alto-rilievo*), the figures project at least half of their natural circumference from the background. Between these two is the demi-relief (half relief or *mezzo-rilievo*).

The lowest degree of relief, in which the projection barely exceeds the thickness of a sheet of paper, is called a crushed relief (*rilievo schiacciato* or *stiacciato*). There is also a relief in reverse, called hollow relief, in which all the carving lies within a hollowed-out area below the surface plane and which, through an illusion of depth and roundness, looks like raised relief. Hollow relief, also called sunk or concave relief (*cavo-rilievo*) and incised relief (*intaglio-rilievo*), are the kind of carving done on gems by the Greeks and Romans. Reliefs may be carved from hard materials or modeled in wet clay, softened wax or plaster. Reliefs are often elements of architectural sculpture.

rosette: a circular carving of foliage or flowers in relief, used as a decorative motif, usually sculptural.

roundel: circular ornament or moulding.

rustification: masonry cut in massive blocks, sometimes in a crude state to give a rich and bold texture.

sarcophagus: a stone coffin, often bearing sculpture, inscriptions and so on.

sculpture-artform: three-dimensional work created in the round that can be seen from all perspectives except the bottom or back (when it is resting or placed down or against a surface, unless hanging from a ceiling or other means) or created as a relief by a sculptor. See **assembly**, **carving**, **modeling** and **welding**.

sculpture in the round: freestanding sculpture that is carved or designed to be viewed on all sides.

spandel: the triangular space between the side of an arch, the horizontal above its apex and the vertical of its springing; the surface between two arches in an arcade.

sphinx: a sculpture in ancient Egypt and ancient Greece having the body of one animal and the head of another, often symbolic of wisdom; the three principal types of sphinxes in the ancient world included the androsphinx, with the body of a lion and the head of a man; the criosphinx, with the body of a lion and the head of a ram; and the heracosphinx, with the body of a lion and the head of a hawk.

sprue: in casting, the entrance hole and main channel in the wall of a mould through which the liquid material (bronze or other metal) is poured. It is joined to the model by smaller channels called gates. The waste material formed by the channel is also called sprue and is cut away after the investment material is removed as the first step to cleaning up a cast metal sculpture.

stabile: a stable abstract sculpture typically executed in such media as sheet metal, wire, iron or stainless steel; opposite of "mobile," a sculpture designed to move through space by winded currents or operated by an electric motor.

steel: medium used for sculpture. Steel is a commercial iron that contains carbon in any amount up to 1.7 percent as an essential alloying constituent, is malleable when under suitable conditions and is distinguished from cast iron by its malleability and lower carbon content.

stele: an upright slab of stone bearing an inscription often used in low-relief sculpture; frequently used as a memorial to a person or event.

stone: 1. cut rock, suitable for carving and building. Stone is one of the traditional materials of the sculptor. It has been carved, drilled and polished since prehistoric times. The most widely available stones for sculpture are alabaster, granite, marble, sandstone and limestone. 2. in the commercial world, any stone except marble.

terra cotta: 1. literally, "cooked earth." Italian for "fired or baked clay" (*terre cuite* in French). The end product of a fired sculpture. 2. the term "terra cotta clay" is often used for any clay suitable for shaping and firing, except for the very fine porcelain clays; popular in the sixteenth century.

terra-cotta: a clayware extensively used as low-relief architectural sculptural panels; fired but unglazed clay, used mainly for monuments in sixteenth century.

volute: a spiral scroll on an Ionic capital.

voussoir: a brick or wedge-shaped stone, forming one of the units of an arch.

weeper: a figure in a recess in a tomb chest, often representing a relative or associate of the person commemorated.

welding: the process of joining together two pieces of metal by fusion. Intense heat is applied by an oxyacetylene torch in gas or oxyacetylene welding and by electrical means in arc welding. Sometimes a filler rod is melted along the joint in the process known as "brazing." The direct welding of two pieces by combining the molten edges is called "fusion welding." It is done at much higher temperatures than soldering and results in stronger, more durable joints. It is used in making direct metal sculpture and comes under the general term of **assembly** (as opposed to **carving** and **modeling**).

Bibliography

BOOKS

Asbury, Christian W. *Richmond: Her Past and Present.* Spartanburg, SC: Reprint Company, 1973.

Babcock, Barbara C., and Tracey L. Kamerer. *A Capitol Collection.* Richmond: Library of Virginia, 2005.

Brown, Beth. *Wicked Richmond.* Charleston, SC: The History Press, 2010.

Byrd, Odell R., Jr. *Richmond, VA: A City of Monuments and Statues.* Richmond, VA: Tarnbuzi Press, 1989.

Case, Keshia A. *Richmond, Virginia: A Walking Tour.* Charleston, SC: Arcadia Publishing, 2010.

Dabney, Virginius. *Richmond.* New York: Doubleday and Company, 1976.

Diggs, Sarah Shields, and John L. Orrock. *Save Outdoor Sculpture!* A Survey of Sculpture in Virginia Compiled. Richmond: Virginia Department of Historic Resources, 1996.

Diggs, Sarah Shields, Richard Guy Wilson and Robert P. Winthrop. *Richmond's Monument Avenue*, Chapel Hill: University of North Carolina Press, 2001.

Dodson, E. Griffith. *The Capitol of the Commonwealth of Virginia at Richmond.* Richmond, VA: Whitten & Sheppardson, 1938.

Doyle, Gale. *A City of Monuments: Historical Highlights Recorded in Metal and Stone.* Richmond, VA: Smart Guidebook, 1989.

Dupree, Judith. *Monuments: America's History in Art and Memory.* New York: Random House, 2007.

Goode, James M. *Washington Sculpture.* Baltimore, MD: Johns Hopkins University Press, 2008.

Griggs, Walter S., Jr. *The Collapse of Richmond's Church Hill Tunnel.* Charleston, SC: The History Press, 2011.

———. *Hidden History of Richmond.* Charleston, SC: The History Press, 2012.

———. "White Ribbons, Temperance, and a Richmond Fountain." *Richmond Guide*, n.d. VCU.

Kimball, Fiske. *The Capitol, 1989.* Richmond: General Assembly of Virginia, 1989.

Kollatz, Harry, Jr. *True Richmond Stories.* Charleston, SC: The History Press, 2007.

Lipton, Seymour. *Recent Works.* London: Marlborough Galleries, 1971.

McGraw, Tyler. *At the Falls.* Chapel Hill: University of North Carolina Press, 1994.

Peters, John O. *Hollywood Cemetery.* Richmond, VA: Richmond History Center, 2010.

Potterfield, Tyler T. *Nonesuch Place.* Charleston, SC: The History Press, 2009.

Ravenal, John B. *Modern and Contemporary Art at the Virginia Museum of Fine Arts.* Charlottesville: University of Virginia Press, 2007.

Robinette, Margaret A. *Outdoor Sculpture Object and Environment.* New York: Whitney Library of Design, 1976.

Ross, R. David. *Welcome to Memory Lane.* Richmond, VA: Kleos Publishing, 2007.

Salmon, Emily J., and John S. Salmon. *Historic Photos of Richmond in the 50s, 60s and 70s.* Richmond, VA: Dietz Press, 2010.

Spears, Katarina M. *Richmond Landmarks.* Charleston, SC: Arcadia Publishing, 2012.

Totty, Dale. *Maritime Richmond.* Charleston, SC: Arcadia Publishing, 2004.

Valentine, Elizabeth Gray. *Dawn to Twilight: Work of Edward V. Valentine.* Richmond, VA: William Byrd Press, 1929.

Wark, R.R. *Sculpture in the Huntington Collection.* Los Angeles, CA: Richie & Simon Anderson, 1959.

BROCHURES

Ezekiel, Moses Jacob. *TH Jefferson.* Richmond: Library of Virginia, n.d.

Main Street Station. Richmond, VA: City of Richmond Office of the Press Secretary, 2003.

A Monumental Evening, Monumental Church. Richmond, VA: Historic Richmond Foundation, 2002.

Richmond's Grand Dame Celebrates Her 90th Birthday. Clifton Forge, VA: Chesapeake & Ohio Historical Society Inc., 1991.

PERIODICALS

African Free Press. April 18, 1987; April 26, 1987; June 2, 1991; June 4, 1991; May 26, 1994; May 27, 1994; May 28, 1994; January 3, 2003; January 4, 2003; January 5, 2003.

Discover Magazine. Section in *Richmond Times-Dispatch*, 2000–2001, 2001–2, 2005–6.

Innsbrook Today. March 2002.

RICHMOND MAIN LIBRARY CLIP FILE

Richmond Newsleader. December 9, 1927; February 11, 1930; February 14, 1930; January 20, 1938; August 10, 1957; June 27, 1958; June 25, 1959; January 16, 1976; April 18, 1978; January 19, 1981; June 7, 1981; June 25, 1986; September 1, 1986; May 16, 1987; May 21, 1987; August 16, 1987; August 21, 1987.

Richmond Times-Dispatch. November 9, 1903; April 2, 1905; August 31, 1905; December 10, 1927; February 11, 1930; October 2, 1938; October 24, 1948; June 27, 1958; October 18, 1959; November 10, 1960; September 2, 1963; June 3, 1968; January 8, 1981; February 23, 1981; February 25, 1983; June 4, 1983; August 31, 1983; May 30, 1994; May 10, 1985; March 20, 1986; August 31, 1986; April 6, 1987; April 18, 1987; April 27, 1987; May 21, 1987; May 30, 1987; October 27, 1991; May 30, 1994; March 16, 1995; September 13, 1995; September 11, 1996; January 30, 1998; May 22, 1999; January 25, 2001; February 12, 2003; March 19, 2003; April 16, 2003; August 13, 2003; May 18, 2005; October 20, 2008; May 30, 2009; January 09, 2012; September 25, 2012; September 28, 2012; November 19, 2012.

Style Weekly Magazine. August 12, 1986; November 25, 1986; September 2, 1997; March 10, 1998; November 6, 2001; April 28, 2002; May 27, 2009; June 20, 2012.

VCU Dentistry Magazine 5, no. 3 (Summer 2007).

Virginia Cavalcade 10, no. 3 (Winter 1960); 27, no. 3 (Winter 1978); 44 (Summer 1994).

Voice 9 (September 8–24, 1995); July 5, 2000.

Index

A

Ampofo-Anti, Kwabena 85
animal fountains 32, 33, 71
Archenima 85
Armstrong, Carl William 114
Arnold, Benedict 111
Asgedom, Araya 85
Ashe, Arthur 10, 70

B

Badger, Viktoria 36
bear monument (Maymont) 74
Bellevue School 116
Bertoia, Harry 28
Biettiger, Wilford D. 91
Boatsman Tower 24
Boyajian, David 113
Boy on Stilts 64
Boy Scouts of America 79, 80
bridge abutment 120
Brown, Henry "Box" 40
Brown's Island 29
Bryan, Joseph 84

Bud and Seed Group 113, 114
Burberl, Casper 93
Burke, Harvey 109
Burke, Milton 109
Byrd Park 34, 69, 70, 78, 100

C

Canal Walk 20, 28, 41
Canova, Antoine 75
carillon 100, 102
Caudill, Ross 65
Chimborazo Park 78
Christopher Newport's Cross 15, 19
Coliseum 81, 91, 108
Columbus, Christopher 70, 71
Confederate Soldiers and Sailors Monument 99
Connecticut 115
Corporate Presence 23
Couper, William 84
Cradle 118

D

dancing man statue 116
Declaration of Independence 49, 52
Deepwater Sponger 31
DiPasquale, Paul 13, 17, 28, 41, 115
Dooley, James Henry 73, 84

E

Earley, Donald 43
Engman, Robert 34
Ezekiel, Moses 43, 51, 100

F

Festival Park 81
First Regiment 89
Follow the Leader (*Children at Play*) 76
Franklin, Benjamin 57
Fraser, James Earle 16
French, David 124
Fulton Gas Works 80
Future 35

G

Gabriel's Rebellion 91
Galanti, Paul 98, 99
Galanti, Phyllis 98, 99
Ginter, Lewis 49, 57, 93, 125
Gissen, Linda 45
Governor's Mansion 51
Grant, Ulysses 120

H

Harpers Ferry 91
Henrico County 13, 105
Henrico High School 116

Hill, Ambrose Powell 92
Hill, Oliver 41, 107
Hippocrates 59, 62
Hotchkiss, Dave 83
Hotchkiss Field 83
Houdon, Jean-Antoine 48, 95
Howitzers 87
Hubard, James 95
Hunt, Gilbert 61
Hutchins, William 113

I

In Pursuit of Growth and Achievement 107, 138

J

James Center 21, 25, 27
James River 15, 19, 20, 25, 26, 34, 74, 75, 78, 93, 115
Jefferson Building 51
Jefferson Hotel 49
Jefferson, Thomas 48, 49, 51

K

Kanawha Canal 21, 25, 27
Kirby-Smith, Maria Juliana 108
Kline, Robert E. 124
Kugel 122

L

Laws, Samuel Spahn 95
Lee, Fitzhugh 93
Lee, Robert E. 77, 79, 92, 94, 120
Lefevre, Greg 25, 26
Legnaioli, Ferruccio 71, 89
Libby Hill Park 99, 104
Lincoln, Abraham 16, 95, 123
Little, Lloyd 22

M

Main Street Station 35, 36, 37
Marshall, John 60
Maymont 70, 73, 74
McGuire, Dr. Hunter Holmes 55, 56
McMahon, Thomas F. 104
Medical College Hospital grill 62
Medical College of Virginia (MCV) 55, 57, 60, 63, 67
Memory 97
Miami University 95
Mill 29
Miller, Larry 13
Miller & Rhoads 109
Mills, Robert 61
Monroe Park 83, 93, 95
Monumental Church 61
Morgan, Charles S. 32
Movieland 126
Mr. Smedley 46

N

Native Americans 57
Newman, John 37
Nicholas, John, Jr. 111

O

Old Dominion Hospital 63
Oliver Hill Courthouse 107
Oliver Hill Detention Center 105

P

Phillips, David 23
Pine Camp 85, 86
police memorial (Sixth Street Market) 108
Ponticello, Charles 31, 67

Powhatan High School 116
Powhatan Stone 80
Proctor, W. Stanley 76

Q

Quadrature 34

R

Rasmussen, William 48
Realmuto, Frank 71
Relaxing at Shields Lake 77
Remembrance ("Rachel Crying for Her Children") 45
Richmond Ambulatory Authority 118
Richmond History Center 19
Richmond Light Infantry Blues 82, 91
River of Tears 42
Robertson, Gilbert 119
Robinson, Bill "Bojangles" 33, 46, 116
Robinson, Bradley 29
Rosati, James 35
Rosenbaum, Allan 118
Roundhouse (Byrd Park) 71, 72

S

Sheppard, William Ludwell 87, 99
Shields Lake 77
shriner holding child statue (Acca Temple) 121
Skyrider 37
Statue of Liberty 10, 79
St. John's Church 116
St. Philip 60
Stutz, Michael 103
Sunday 105

T

Tableith 67
temperance 71
Thin Blue Line 103
three bears sculpture in MCV 57
Three Graces 75
Trani, Eugene P. 65
Tredegar Iron Works 20, 21, 30,
    124
Triangle (Slavery Reconciliation
    Statue) 38
Trotti, John Boone 125
Truth and Beauty 65

V

Valentine, Edward V. 49, 94
Valentine Museum 13
Van Lew, Elizabeth 116
Vigil 95, 96
Viktoria's Station 35
Virginia Capital Trail 113
Virginia Commonwealth University
    13, 15, 55, 65, 87, 107, 118
Virginia Historical Society 41, 47
Virginia Mourning Her Dead (VMI) 43
Virginia Museum of Fine Arts 13,
    72

W

Walker, Maggie Lena 118
War Horse 47
Washington, George 16, 20, 49, 84,
    89, 94
Washington Monument 95
West Point Military Academy 92
White House of the Confederacy
    44, 57, 124
Wickham, Williams Carter 85, 95
Willard, Frances 72

Winds Up 22
Witt, John T. Jack 46
World War I 100, 102
World War II 85, 97

About the Author and Photographer

Bob Layton, a resident of Glen Allen, Virginia, retired from a successful insurance sales career in 1993. During his tenure, he served as president of both the Richmond and Virginia Life Underwriters Associations and served on several national committees. He was also the lobbying arm of the state association for a number of years and a life member of the Million Dollar Roundtable.

In retirement, Bob has found a variety of life's fun things to do. His interests range from volunteering, traveling, writing and reading to an occasional political dabble. Bob has written more than 150 articles on a variety of subjects with thirty-five different publications. His play *George Washington Wept Here* has not met expectations but was a rewarding activity.

The research for putting pen to paper has provided the material for his more than two hundred lectures on travel, history, monuments and animals. He has appeared before a variety of audiences giving programs in national parks, retirement facilities, libraries and historical societies, as well as for Elderhostel and at the University of Richmond. He numbers teaching sixth grade in Beijing, China, as one of the most rewarding retirement experiences.

Bob has traveled to all fifty states and visited more than seventy-five countries. Walking across the Grand Canyon, climbing the Great Wall of

China and weekly tennis have contributed to an exciting withdrawal from the workplace.

This book is the culmination of several years' worth of gathering information and photos of Richmond statues—more a labor of love than occupation for photographer Phil Riggan. He has been discovering Richmond as a writer and photographer for two decades, especially with the extra inspiration and motivation gained from having his son, Mitchell, and daughter, Carly, go with him. The James River is their favorite playground, but exploring Richmond's history—especially statues, monuments and sculpture—has been a great way for his wife, Trish, and him to keep the kids away from electronics and get them outdoors and active.

He believes that if you love public art, support the effort to preserve and maintain these works through Save Our Statues. Find more about SOS through the Enrichmond Foundation (serving Richmond's people, parks and public spaces) at enrichmond.org.

Visit us at
www.historypress.net

....

This title is also available as an e-book

CPSIA information can be obtained
at www.ICGtesting.com
Printed in the USA
LVHW080016190720
661014LV00015B/368